Seniors GET YOUR DUCKS IN A ROW

PROTECT YOUR NEST

Annette Fisher • Debra S Gross • Robert Howe
Marie Sayour • Marla Loughran • Mary Maroney

Illustrated by Robert Bello

ISBN: 0692202528
ISBN 13: 9780692202524

Library of Congress Control Number: 2017900214
Golden Maturity Inc., Brooklyn, NEW YORK

Edited by Joanne Naiman

For Quantity Purchases of This Book Contact:
Golden Maturity Inc.
4210 Surf Avenue
Brooklyn NY 11224
annette@GoldenMaturity.com
347-291-7479

To set up a Book Signing, Educational Forum for your company or Fundraiser for your organization please contact:
Golden Maturity Inc.
4210 Surf Avenue
Brooklyn NY 11224
annette@GoldenMaturity.com
347-291-7479

Library of Congress Control Number: 2017900214
Golden Maturity Inc., Brooklyn, NEW YORK
Fisher Annette
Seniors Get Your Ducks In A Row
Protect Your Nest

Limited Liability Disclaimer/Disclaimer of Warranty
The Publisher and Authors make no representation or warranties in respect to the accuracy, completeness, or time sensitivity of information, as it pertains to the contents of this work. Information on what works in one state may not work in another. Also, each person's set of circumstances tends to vary making the recipe for the solution to an individual need, a custom formula, so to speak. You should always seek the advice of a professional advisor with expertise in the area in which you are looking for help. *All of the authors of this work are offering a complimentary initial consultation.*

This book is for seniors, as well as the families, caretakers and friends of seniors. It's our mission to provide the knowledge seniors need to keep up with the constantly changing times in which we live. Seniors are living longer and having to stretch their dollars further. We hope the insight in this book will provide you with at least the sprinkling of knowledge you will need to get started on your journey to protecting your family nest. In addition, the stories told throughout this book are intended to either inspire seniors to take charge of their lives or to be made aware of what they may not know. One of the funniest things about knowledge is sometimes you don't know what you don't know until you know it. So, we invite you to read on and enjoy the journey through our eyes and ears, as we enlighten you with real life stories, only the names and places may have changed.

Live Well, Laugh Lots and Live Long!

DID YOU EVER STOP AND WONDER

Did you ever stop and wonder
How time has passed so fast?
We hold on to our memories
We don't give up our past.

We look into a mirror
And the face there that we see
Is usually our parent
For us it cannot be.

We still feel in our twenties-
Age thirty years at best
We don't understand why we move so slow
Or often have to rest.

Aging is a process
One we all go through
We know we cannot stop it
No matter what we do.

So live life to the fullest
Enjoy each and every day
Our time here is a precious gift
What more can I say!

Mary Maroney

PRAISE

Welcome, readers! Within you will find a compilation of information that is meant to help you meet the challenges of growing old. I am sure you will find each of the contributors not only knowledgeable but also caring and dedicated to our aging population.

Each of the contributors has worked hard to make a difference in the lives of older adults. The stories they have portrayed will shed some light on what you can do to prepare for your future. All of the authors are members of PESID, People Empowering Seniors Independence & Dignity, which gives seniors an avenue in which to voice their concerns as well as their accomplishments to a larger population. It is our hope that you will absorb and make use of the information within.

Frances Picone, RSM
Director of Services for Older Adults
Lutheran Family Health Centers

I have worked with seniors and their families for many years in my social work practice. People have often come to me feeling stressed and overwhelmed, looking for support and a direction on how to proceed in dealing with the challenging issues facing elders.

In my professional opinion, I believe that "Seniors Get Your Ducks In A Row" is an excellent starting point in this process of gaining knowledge of the needs of seniors. It is a comprehensive compilation of resources including contributions from experts in their fields covering topics such as: finances, reverse mortgages, real estate, health, nutrition, and elder law. All contributors are members of The PESID Organization (People Empowering Seniors' Independence & Dignity). This book includes a number of wonderful examples of how having proper information leads to successful outcomes.

I highly recommend this book as a valuable educational tool in aiding seniors and their loved ones.

Denise P. Levine, L.C.S.W.

INTRODUCTION

The contributors to this book are all members of PESID (People Empowering Seniors Independence & Dignity). PESID is a networking group dedicated to the idea of building resources for seniors.

PESID is a resource group where seniors and their families can find incredible information and service providers. PESID members who care for or work with seniors, understand the unique problems of seniors. PESID members offer a myriad of resources and merchant discounts to enhance the quality of seniors' lives. You should do some vetting when hiring people as PESID doesn't guarantee the services of members. You can and should ask for references.

Each of the contributors to this book assists seniors in different ways, from health to housing to finances. Each contributor is caring and takes the time to listen to their senior clients' specific needs. And each has the experience to solve the particular challenges seniors face.

Annette Fisher has worked in the mortgage industry for the past 18 years and for more than 12 years has devoted herself to working with seniors. As a Reverse Mortgage Loan Originator NMLS 67606, Annette is very involved with seniors, the originating, and processing of applications and she is the liaison between, seniors interested in reverse mortgages, attorneys, title companies, as well as business partners of the firm. At the same time, Annette is also a real estate salesperson therefore she has a broader view than most when it comes to the question, do I stay or do I go?

In addition, Annette is the founder of Golden Maturity, Inc., whose mission it is to educate as well as provide information to seniors and their families. Also, Golden Maturity Inc. is the publishing company for this book. The company's WalletICE™ is a free card for seniors to carry, listing their vital medical information.

Debra S. Gross is a registered dietitian, a certified dietitian nutritionist, and a certified diabetes educator specializing in helping seniors control their diabetes. She offers seniors "user friendly" advice on how to eat healthy, taking into consideration a senior's lifestyle and food preferences.

Robert Howe, a wills, trusts, and estates attorney, is celebrating his law firm's 36th anniversary. He assists his many senior clients with devising orderly legal plans that ensure their financial, health care and testamentary wishes are carried out.

Dr. Marla Loughran, a second-generation chiropractor, offers her senior patients gentle exercises and treatments to relieve pain and keep them as mobile and functional as long as possible.

Mary Maroney, RN, MSN, is a co-founder in Maxireturn, which is in the forefront of helping doctor's offices and hospitals implement standardized electronic medical records so that seniors (and all other patients) will be assured that their complete medical histories will be preserved.

Marie Sayour is a principal in RN Staffing Solutions, LLC, which provides non-medical companions to seniors in homes, hospitals and nursing home settings to keep seniors safe, fed and offers them a sense of social connection.

By sharing the information in this book, we hope we will be educating seniors and their families thus enriching seniors' lives, allowing them more independence and dignity. PESID members currently meet in Brooklyn, Nassau County and Staten Island. PESID will be starting meetings in other geographic locations as membership expands. Meetings are open to seniors and their families whom we encourage to attend as well as professionals serving seniors. A free PESID Discount Card is also available for seniors. For all of us, it is also a great night out, sharing, and enjoying, LOL. For more information on PESID, People Empowering Seniors Independence & Dignity, you can go to PESID.com or call Annette Fisher at 347-291-7479.

ONWARD BY STATE SENATOR MARTIN J. GOLDEN

This book, Seniors Get Your Ducks In A Row, co-authored by Annette Fisher, Debra Gross, Robert Howe, Marie Sayour, Marla Loughran, and Mary Maroney, explains several aspects of life as a senior. The book, which is written by professionals who have a great amount of experience in their field, is meant to help seniors take advantage of opportunities available to them, from in the housing market to making a will to health concerns, by clearly explaining the given area, giving several examples and contact information for the authors for more information.

In the first section, Getting a Clean Bill of Legal Health, written by Howe, explains the significance of a will to seniors who want their property to be in certain hands after their death. The benefits of a will and how one should be acquired are given in this section, helping to clear up any confusion that many might have. Showing the negative effects of not having a will while still alive and mentally capable of writing one as well, Howe excellently explains this area to readers.

The following, Moving Forward in Reverse, by Fisher, is meant to explain reverse mortgages to readers. She, a Senior Advisor and Reverse Mortgage Loan Originator at Fort Funding Corp., tells seniors the truth about reverse mortgages, as there are many misconceptions. By using examples, Fisher teaches a reader, who's eligible for a reverse mortgage, and how it can be obtained. If a reverse mortgage is not right for a senior she will let them know. Fisher also a NYS licensed real estate salesperson explains some of the housing choices that may be of interest to them, or things they may need to take care of if they are looking to sell the home. See her real estate chapter "My Home Is My Castle" for more on real estate.

Section three, written by Sayour, explains how to obtain a companion for seniors, whether needed because of a physical or mental disability, or just because one is in need of someone to talk to. By giving statistics of how many people are in need of a companion because of disabilities and giving examples of cases she has dealt with in the past, Sayour, Principal at RN Staffing Solutions, LLC., explains to seniors that they can get someone to help them if they need someone.

Healthy Eating: The Good, the Bad, and the Ugly, by Gross, a Dietitian, tells seniors how healthy eating benefits them as they get older. Proving many misconceptions about diabetes, which is common amongst seniors, to be wrong, Gross helps show seniors that serious health problems can be avoided in several ways with healthy eating.

Following that is Naturally Healing from Pain, at Any Age, written by Loughran, explains how important chiropractic care is for seniors. By explaining this in layman's terms, Loughran makes it easy for readers to understand.

Next, Electronic Medical Records: What Will They Mean to Us? by Maroney tells seniors the pros and cons of a new idea, electronic medical records. This is meant to spread one's medical information worldwide to any medical professional, in order to make transferring information easier.

Finally, WalletICE™, Can Save Your Life, written by Fisher, encourages readers to use WalletICE™, a vital tool that can help doctors obtain important medical information about the carrier in case of emergency.

Seniors, Get Your Ducks In A Row is an excellent resource for seniors who have questions about the rest of their life, written by professionals in their fields and contains several pieces of important information.

State Senator Martin J. Golden
7408 5th Avenue
Brooklyn, NY 11209
O: 718-238-6044
F: 718-238-6170

SENIORS, GET YOUR DUCKS IN A ROW: PROTECT YOUR NEST -- BASED ON TRUE STORIES" -- A BOOK REVIEW OF THE ESSENTIAL HANDBOOK FOR NAVIGATING THROUGH THE LATER MATURITY YEARS

by Harold Egeln

Perhaps for the first time there is now an essential, complete, comprehensive and compassionate handbook from leading experienced professionals who work closely with older adults in a variety of aspects of navigating through the later maturity years that presents advice, help and resources, spanning areas such as health, nutrition, dwelling choices, legal matters and more.

The large audience for this remarkable and inspiring book includes seniors, their families, caregivers, friends of seniors and health and medical professionals, and the curious general public. It has an upbeat approach, with the words, "Live well, laugh lots and live long!"

I am immensely excited and gratified, as many readers will be, that "Seniors, Get Your Ducks In A Row: Protect Your Nest -- Based on True Stories" is now out there with its special emphasis on empowering seniors with invaluable knowledge, co-authored by six amazing talented professionals who are leaders in their fields, and whose jobs intersect. All six are members and driving forces of a remarkable organization that produced this book. PESID, People Empowering Seniors Independence & Dignity, a network of professionals working to better the lives of seniors, started in Brooklyn and also in Richmond and Nassau Counties with open network meetings, was founded by leading senior advocate Annette Fisher, founder of Golden Maturity, Inc. which published this book.

This reviewer covered the initial PESID gatherings, assigned to him as a staff reporter for the "Brooklyn Daily Eagle" newspaper. The PESID professionals, some of whom I know, work cooperatively to not only provide and grow resources for seniors in their search for independence and dignity, but to show critically informed directions for them.

And "Seniors, Get Your Ducks In A Row" is their treasure trove of specific information and accumulated knowledge for taking actions to maximize people's richly experienced lives. The six professionals use true stories with people's names changed to illustrate their work explained clearly in their chapters.

In the first chapter "Getting a Clean Bill of Legal Health," estate, trust and wills attorney Robert Howe, with 36 years of legal experience, writes of examples of the making and necessity of wills, living wills, appointing health care proxies and people with the power of attorney, while clearing up misconceptions. "I always advise my clients to make executors' jobs easier (by) sitting down with (them) and tell them where all your records are located," he wrote. Howe gives the clearest, best explained and most informed account of the four areas of his work that I have ever read. In citing true stories, he shows how seniors can organize "their legal life in order to enjoy their personal life."

In her "Moving Forward in Reverse," chapter, senior advisor Annette Fisher, a reverse mortgage consultant and real estate salesperson and founder of Golden Maturity, Inc., tells of the biggest benefit of reverse mortgages in that there "are no monthly payments of principal and interest as long as the borrower remains in their home as their primary residence" and makes regular payments, for real estate taxes and home owners insurance.

Most critically now, she discusses the changes announced in October 2013 regarding a U.S. Department of Housing and Urban Development (HUD) asset test that took effect starting April 27, 2015 according to the HUD mortgagee letter. In her work with seniors, Fisher wrote, "I know the right questions to ask. I always want to involve you, your family and other advisors to get the best possible solution for you."

In telling her stories and how not to be pressured into moves that are not their own preferences, Fisher said that reverse mortgages give people few limitations and open "all sorts of possibilities for her clients," freeing their imaginations to explore those possibilities.

In "Home Care, Home Is Where the Heart Is," Marie Sayour, a principal of RN Staffing Solutions, LLC providing quality, trained, reliable and screened home caregivers companion service tailored to individuals, aims to "give pleasure to a senior's day" as told in her chapter.

One story that illuminates dramatic positive possibilities, "Giving a Norwegian Gem Back Her Luster," tells of a mentally alert, very bright 92-year-old woman who suffered from a fall, dulling her life almost to a standstill. With a caregiver's special attention to the woman, Sayour writes that "she blossomed... the change was overwhelming." "There are," she wrote, "a myriad of ways that a companion can make a difference. In her chapter, she writes that its purpose is "to demonstrate that seniors are not alone and there is help available, no matter what the situation might be."

A life-affirming story of food, glorious healthy food to be specific, is told in the "Nutrition, Road to Longevity" chapter by Debra Gross, a Registered Dietitian/Nutritionist , a New York State   Certified Dietitian Nutritionist and a Certified Diabetes Educator for nearly to 20 years. Debra points out a growing epidemic of Type II diabetes and obesity plaguing Americans, with at least a 36 percent increase for seniors 67 years and older within that last decade, as noted in the literature.

Dietitian Gross helps seniors to create individualized nutrition plans that "give a person a voice in any meal plan, and with that plan in place, that "diabetes is not a life sentence, but can be controlled well."

Back hurt? Neck hurt? In "Chiropractor: Naturally Healing from Pain, At Any Age" Dr. Marla Loughran looks at "Natural healing at any age: by looking at parts of the spine involved with the onset and worsening affects of osteoarthritis and other degenerative spinal conditions common to seniors." Medicines may help but mask the problems. What it takes is a manageable method to make seniors stay active, restore, and keep good posture and nutrition.

One of her stories is that of a 63-year-old longshoreman, then working part-time, who was in the early stages of increasing pain and being stressed out by it. Through her "gentle, natural health care" of chiropractic work, his energy and vitality were revived. Loughran wrote, "We emphasize that exercise is imperative for everyone to maintain healthy cardiovascular and respiratory systems, (and) great for reducing stress."

The advantages of "EMR, Electronic Medical Records -- Helps Doctors Care For You," the chapter by Mary Maroney, a co-founder of MaxiReturn Services, tells how, with her well-trained staff, she and her team help provide choices of an EHR/EMR system that fits right for senior clients and doctors.

MaxiReturn assists hospitals and physician offices in converting to electronic formats for medical records, training and support hospital staff in this growing and essential computerized service and makes life easier for both doctors and patients. Maroney wrote, "We work with everyone on this push into the electronic medical record-keeping frontier."

At book's end, Fisher is back with the most compact, convenient and carry-able paper anybody can keep in their wallet or purse: a WalletICE™ card that folds out with space to place vital medical information in case of medical emergencies, for ambulance and ER personnel, and doctors. The information space includes places for medical history, prescriptions, allergies, over-the-counter remedies and pharmacy location.

This "snapshot of your medical history," wrote Fisher, "might even save your life...and can help doctors and hospitals diagnose your emergency situations." I have found it invaluable in the few unexpected trips by ambulance to emergency rooms in the past few years, thanks to Fisher's innovation, I highly recommend it.

As I do this, too and with great emphasis, with this absolutely invaluable, essential and thoroughly informative book chockfull of knowledge you can bank on, with its truly warmly-told human hallmarks thanks to its highly knowledgeable and experienced authors who are members of PESID and who are working together TO HELP YOU!

For information on purchasing the book, visit www. PESID.com or contact Annette Fisher at 1-347-291-7479. Also can be found at SeniorsGetYourDucksInARow.com

---

Reviewer Harold Egeln is a longtime professional journalist who has written thousands of articles and hundreds of columns for three decades. He was most recently a staff general assignment reporter for the Brooklyn Daily Eagle and Bay Ridge Eagle, and before that a staff reporter for the Brooklyn Chamber of Commerce's newspaper, the Courier Life and Home Reporter/Brooklyn Spectator News. He served as a media aide and speechwriter at NY Council-member Vincent Gentile's office, and was the full-time executive director (1984-1989) of the nonprofit Metro-NYC Peace Council for a SANE Nuclear Policy (now Peace Action) with 7,000 members and a dozen chapters in the city, the NYC office of a large national organization. He has a lifetime history as a volunteer leader in community-action peace and environmental organizations, also publishing their newsletters and appeared on dozens of television and radio programs. He is president of the NYC chapter of National Space Society.

Egeln is currently a free-lance writer and is a contributing reporter and photographer for the "Living With Style in Southwest Brooklyn" quarterly magazine published by The Networking Productions Group based in Bay Ridge, Brooklyn. Born and raised in Essex County, New Jersey, he has lived in Bay Ridge since 1982, and has written hundreds of articles on senior issues, including most recently a review of the first book, an inspiring and powerful autobiography, by an 82-year-old notable retired cabaret performer, stage and Broadway singer and actress, now working on two novels.

TABLE OF CONTENTS

ATTORNEY

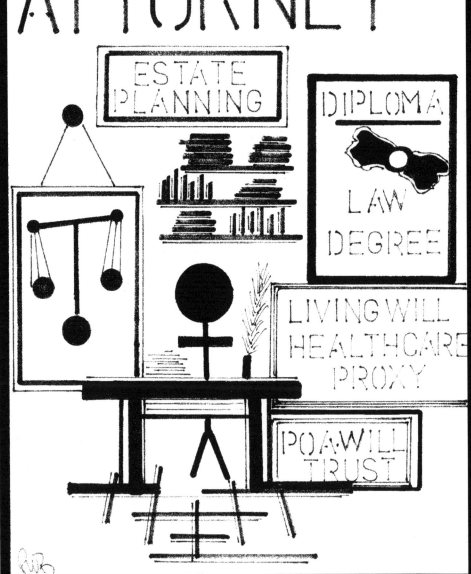

ESTATE PLANNING

DIPLOMA
LAW
DEGREE

LIVING WILL
HEALTHCARE
PROXY

POA WILL
TRUST

GETTING A CLEAN BILL OF LEGAL HEALTH

Not a week goes by in my legal practice that I don't get calls from people inquiring about a will. They have all sorts of misconceptions about the necessity of having one and how to create one. They even tell me that the nice spokesman on television says it's easy for them to do themselves! Yes there are computer programs, internet services and Staples forms for wills, but it's not that simple.

In truth, most people need a will yesterday, and there are many legal pitfalls to "trying this at home." You use an auto mechanic to fix your car, an accountant to do your taxes, a doctor to diagnose you. It makes equally good sense to have an attorney advise you about your entire estate!

And wills alone do not provide complete legal coverage. In addition, people need powers of attorney, health care proxies and living wills to protect them throughout their lives. Once you've acquired these four documents, you have what I refer to as a *Clean Bill of Legal Health*.

WILLS

Do you have a will? Between half and two-thirds of American adults don't.

1

SENIORS GET YOUR DUCKS IN A ROW

Do you need one? Only if you answer yes to any of the questions below:

1. Do you care who gets your property when you die?
2. Do you care who gets your money when you die?
3. Do you care who is appointed guardian of your minor children when you die?
4. Do you care who manages your estate?

A will dictates the manner in which your property will be divided and names a business manager called an executor. It is signed by you, the maker, called the testator, in front of two witnesses who also sign it.

If a will isn't prepared by an experienced attorney, there are several risks you run that can result in your wishes not being carried out. For one thing, beneficiaries are prohibited from acting as witnesses – if they do they will lose their bequests. (You should use disinterested parties as witnesses.)

As a testator, you have to say you are signing your will, you know its contents, and you have affirmatively asked the people to act as witnesses. When you go to an attorney, he or she makes sure all the legal requirements are met, including the ceremonial aspects of creating a will– from the proper use of language to the proper procedure in regards to the signing.

In terms of contents, you should sit down with your attorney for a careful discussion on what you wish to bequeath and whom you want to benefit. Wills can range from relatively simple expressions of your wishes: *I leave everything to my four children,* to very complex schemes with trusts and tax savings clauses.

They can also be very specific: You can draw up a will leaving your gold ring to Mary. Or in the alternative very general: "I leave my entire estate in equal shares to my children." I always tell my clients that some specific items might not be around years later, so general bequeaths are usually the better way to go. (A red Cadillac may be sold and replaced with a green Lincoln. A bank account at Citibank may be transferred to Chase.)

And here's another suggestion--don't get so bogged down in the minutiae of your estate assets that you lose the big picture. One client came to me with two pages of what to do with specific personal items in his house. When I asked what he wanted to do with the house itself and his bank accounts, he told me he hadn't decided!

I advised him to follow my general rule–decide what you want to do about your biggest assets first. A letter can be written about what to do with the small items and given to the executor, who will divide these up.

Wills can make bequests to your favorite charities or to people you want to benefit in specific amounts or percentages. When both spouses are alive, they generally make wills leaving everything to each other and upon the death of the second spouse, to their children.

Spouses want to consider who will be a guardian of any minor children if both parents pass away. They will also have to decide who will be their alternate executor (if they choose each other as executor). Many times they select their oldest child or the child who has the best business sense.

The executor is the business manager of the estate. That person hires the attorney, the accountant and any other professionals. The executor receives a small percentage as a fee for their services or they can waive the fee. Sometimes the job of executor can be thankless, because the paramount thought on the minds of the beneficiaries is when they can get their money.

The executor has the responsibility of locating and collecting the assets, paying bills and taxes, and then distributing the balance. Sometimes the entire process takes about a year. It is hard for some beneficiaries to hear they have to wait for the process to unfold this slowly.

The point is to choose an executor, who can handle the pressure of pleasing beneficiaries, is responsible and has a good business sense. I always advise my clients to make their executor's job easier. Sit down and have a discussion with your executor (who can be your spouse) and give him or her an informal inventory of all your assets and debts and where all your records are located. After you die, your executor shouldn't have to go hunting for bankbooks, etc. Make sure to include the account numbers/names and location of the documents in your discussion such as:

1. All bank books
2. Deeds to real property and titles to cars
3. Tax returns, (taxes owed/taxes paid)
4. All pension accounts, and brokerage accounts

The point is that estate planning doesn't mean just making a will and forgetting about it. It means thinking not only about whom you want to benefit from your estate but also how to make the executor's job as easy as possible in distributing that estate.

If you do end up like the majority of Americans without a will, the state steps in and decides who will inherit your assets. The state has thus made in essence a default plan called intestacy. It is more costly and takes longer than distributing assets under a will.

Your property doesn't then go to the state, but it might go to people you didn't want to benefit, such as a cousin you haven't seen for decades or might have never even met. The state also has a pecking order for those who can manage your estate, (known as an administrator). Once again this person may not be the one you prefer.

Few situations without a will turn out as happily as my most memorable case. Years ago I represented an estate of approximately three million dollars. The decedent had no will and probably no idea he had such a large estate. He died of malnourishment eating dog food near the end of his life. His relatives in Europe inherited his entire estate intestate. When I visited them in Europe, they all asked me about their cousin, whom they had never met. The relatives were all humble, needy and extremely grateful for the windfall.

Lastly you may never need to use a will if the assets you own have someone else's name on them. The simplest examples are a joint bank account, a jointly owned house and/or a life insurance policy that states a beneficiary. Let me impart a few words of caution, though.

If you open a joint bank account with someone, it should be a person you trust one-hundred-percent because this person has the right to take out all the money in the account while you're still alive. The better option for the bank account is to have it in your name and in trust for the second person. This person then has no ownership interest until your death.

Some clients want me to put the names of their children on their deeds because they want their children to have their home after they die. I advise against this. Instead, I suggest they can accomplish the same results by executing a simple will.

Once you put other people's names on your deed, you are in effect becoming financial partners with them. And the consequences can be disastrous. If your children get into financial trouble, you now possess an asset that their creditors can go after. Add also the spouses of your children, and you are now part of a small real estate company. And its asset is your house! Deed transfers may have a place in certain situations but should only be considered after serious consultation with an attorney and an accountant.

You have spent more than half a century accumulating your wealth–you should spend a few days providing how your estate will be distributed when you are no longer around. I even tell some clients who agonize about their wills to spend every penny now, so that neither they nor their beneficiaries will have any cares. I was struck recently by a news report of the wealthiest man in England, who told his children that he was not leaving them anything because he didn't want to burden them with the job of managing such wealth!

But seriously, take time to look at your holdings, how they are titled, whom you want to benefit, and how much you want to give your beneficiaries. You will have provided an orderly plan for your estate, and you will cut down your executor's stress in administering your estate. Consult an attorney who is an authority on trusts and estates to put your wishes and thoughts into a properly written plan called a will.

LIVING WILL

Something even more precious than your property is your own life. We all wish to have control over how we live, even as we approach death.

A Living Will is a written document that states your wishes regarding your end-of- life health care if you become mentally and/or physically incapable of expressing those wishes. It is used by those who want to declare whether or not they want withheld certain medical treatments that prolong the process of dying.

I advise my clients that they should have a living will not just for their sake but also to relieve a potential burden on their children. For example sometimes siblings are at odds over whether or not to take their mother off a respirator or take out a feeding tube, and one child expresses the inevitable thought: *I just wish we knew what mom would have wanted.*

If one side of a family insists on "pulling the plug" and another wishes to keep their loved one on life support, New York state courts recognize a living will as your end-of-life wishes and consider it a factor in deciding which medical course should be taken—even if the courts don't consider a living will as strong a legal determinant as a contract.

The living will, which generally requires two witnesses, begins by stating that the person is of sound mind and is making a statement as a directive to be followed if he or she becomes permanently unable to participate in decisions regarding his or her own medical care. And though many people want to make clear their objection to unwanted medical measures in advance, others use a living will to express their wish to have all available life-sustaining treatments administered.

How specific should you be in your living will? Your living will should express your general wishes, but it can also be as specific as you want. It might generally state that the attending physician should *withhold or withdraw treatment that merely prolongs dying,* if you have *an incurable or irreversible mental or physical condition with no reasonable expectation of recovery.*

Specifically it can state that a person doesn't want *cardiac resuscitation, mechanical respiration, artificial nutrition and/or hydration or antibiotics.* It can direct that treatment be limited to measures to keep you comfortable and to relieve pain. You can specifically state that you want *maximum pain relief, even if that hastens death.*

If you have definite desires or preferences as to medical treatment under certain circumstances, it is important to spell them out both in the living will and in discussions with your health care agent and physician. This written and oral evidence helps ensure that your wishes and values will be respected when you can no longer make such judgments on your own behalf.

With such rapid advances in medicine, it is difficult for the layperson to ever know what is currently available in terms of end-of-life treatment. A client of mine made a good suggestion to seek out a family member or friend in the medical field to advise you as to all of the new technologies in order to make an informed decision about what you do or don't want given to you.

Living wills are not without their detractors. Some criticize them as too uncertain and unable to keep up with modern medical developments. You should consult with your physician first and your attorney second to ensure your living will expresses what you want. Contradictory and vague directives will negate a living will's purpose–to have your wishes clearly conveyed.

And unfortunately, don't think of yourself as too young or too healthy to make these decisions or have these discussions. Remember the case of Terri Schiavo, a young woman on life support caught in a tug of war between her spouse and her family. No one knows what tomorrow brings. It is best that you and your loved ones are prepared.

HEALTH CARE PROXY

Unlike living wills, in which a written document outlines your end-of-life wishes, you sometimes need another person to make medical decisions for you–even if it's just for a brief period. As we live longer and medical procedures advance, the question arises as to who will make your medical choices if you are not capable of deciding. In the last few decades, states have been passing laws allowing an individual to delegate the decision making to a family member or friend, acting as your health care agent.

GETTING A CLEAN BILL OF LEGAL HEALTH

The New York Health Care Proxy Law allows you to appoint someone you trust as your health care agent. It is like a power of attorney for health care decisions. Your agent also has the authority to decide how your wishes apply as your medical condition changes. Hospitals, doctors and other health care providers must follow your agent's decisions as if they were your own.

Even when you have a health care proxy, you have the right to make all your health care decisions for yourself as long as you are able to do so. Treatment cannot be given to you or stopped if you object, nor will your agent have any power to object. A doctor determines when you aren't able to make decisions and it becomes appropriate for your agent to step in.

I advise my clients that it is imperative to have a health care proxy. For example, if you are taken to a hospital in a coma, the doctors look to someone to make decisions about the type of treatment you will receive. Absent any health care agent or family member, the hospital will follow its own protocols, which may include treatments/procedures you would not have wanted.

A health care proxy should be drawn up by your lawyer. It doesn't need to be notarized, but it should be witnessed by two people (who are not the designated health care agent). Hospitals often have their own forms, which you execute if you are able to at the time. You should always bring your form to the hospital and ask them if they have their own which they require.

You may allow your agent to make all health care decisions or only certain ones. The proxy gives the person you choose as your agent the authority to make all health care decisions for you, including the decision to remove or provide life-sustaining treatment, unless you say otherwise. And you decide if you want your agent to be given instructions that he or she must follow. (Unless your agent reasonably knows your wishes about artificial nutrition and hydration, he or she will not be allowed to refuse or consent to these measures for you.)

The most challenging question you–with your lawyer's and family's assistance–will be answering is: Who is the ideal person to select as your health care agent?

There are a few basic legal requirements:

1. The agent must be 18 years of age or older
2. You can choose a family member or close friend. However, if you select a doctor, he or she will have to decide to either act as your agent or as your attending doctor but can't do both.
3. If you are a patient or resident of a hospital, nursing home or mental hygiene facility, there are restrictions about naming someone who works for that facility as your agent. Ask your facility for information about those restrictions.
4. If you select your husband or wife as your health care agent and you later divorce, your former spouse can not remain as your health care agent

unless you update your current form to explicitly state that they should remain your agent, or designate them in a new health care proxy.

Aside from legal requirements, there are common sense considerations in choosing your health care agent. Choose someone who knows your general wishes, lifestyle and outlook on life. If you haven't seen someone in years or know him or her only casually, this person is obviously not the best choice. And you may be close to someone emotionally, but if he or she lives far away, that person won't make a good health care agent. You need someone who can easily reach the place where you are being cared for.

It surprises me every time I hear a story about a health care agent who only learns he or she has been designated when a hospital informs them that they must start making medical decisions! Before appointing anyone as your health care agent, discuss it with the person to make sure he or she is willing to act as your agent. And just as importantly, you should discuss with that person the types of treatments you want and don't want, and your general outlook on your own medical care. If you are someone who believes in being taken off life supports, pick as your agent a friend or relative you know has the resolve to make this type of difficult decision.

You should appoint an alternate agent if your health care agent is unavailable, unable or unwilling to act when decisions must be made. Joint or co-agents are unadvisable because they may disagree on treatment, and thus no directives would be given.

It is easy to cancel your health care proxy, to change the person you have chosen as your health care agent or to change any instructions or limitations you have included in the document. Simply fill out a new one. In addition, you may indicate that your health care proxy expires on a specified date or if certain events occur.

Give a copy to your agent, your doctor, your attorney and family members or close friends. Keep a copy in your wallet or purse or with other important papers, but not in a location no one can access, such as a safe deposit box.

Your agent is expected to make decisions based on specific knowledge of your wishes. If your agent does not know what you would want in a particular situation, they should try to infer your wishes based on their knowledge of you as a person and on your values related to quality of life. If your agent lacks this knowledge, decisions must be in your best interest. Generally, the more confident and informed your agent is that his or her decisions accurately reflect your wishes, the easier these decisions will be for your agent to make.

POWER OF ATTORNEY

A power of attorney is a powerful document. It's something you can't live without—but you don't want to live with, unless you can do so safely.

A power of attorney is also a simple document. It says: "I appoint John Smith to act on my behalf." Originally conceived to allow someone to act as your agent when you were out of town, ill or even in a coma, the power of attorney now has many benefits. Sadly, some agents take advantage of those who grant them a power of attorney. But new state laws have been cutting down on abuses, and there are ways you can protect yourself before you grant someone the power to act in your name.

Let's first focus on the positive uses of the power of attorney. These are just some examples of how useful a power of attorney can be to you or a loved one:

1) Seniors or others homebound or hospitalized can designate a trusted friend or relative as an agent to do their banking and relatively simple financial transactions.

2) The power of attorney can even be used to sell or refinance your house—if for example, you are unable to be present at the closing sale of your home, you can send an agent.

3) Medical insurers typically won't talk to anyone but a policyholder about his or her coverage, but what if you're in a coma and being denied benefits? A power of attorney gives someone else the right to talk to the insurer on your behalf.

4) Another beneficial use of the POA is in giving away or spending down money. Medicaid and estate

tax laws can be minimized with proper gifting. Generally, these issues only arise when a senior is in a nursing home and the agent at the eleventh hour has to do some planning.

All of the new powers of attorney are called durable, meaning that the agent can still use them if the principal becomes incompetent. However, a person must be competent to initially grant the power. I cannot tell you how many clients ask me for a power of attorney after their parent has become incompetent. I have to say that I'm sorry, but it's too late. (A costly and involved Guardianship proceeding may be the only way to help the parent then.) For the few dollars it costs to do the POA, the savings could be in the thousands. That's why I always advise my clients to have their power of attorney drawn up and just hold onto it until they need it.

The most important advice I can give for safely using a power of attorney is to only give it to someone you trust 110 percent. In addition, a power of attorney doesn't have to grant limitless power to your agent. You can give the agent power to do only one specific task, i.e. "Sell my house on 81st street." Or you can limit the duration that the power of attorney is in effect, for example "until 2016," or even "until I come back from my September 2016 trip to Florida." (It might be extremely helpful to you to give your children a power of attorney while you are on vacation so they can write checks to pay your bills.)

Sometimes banks, for their own protection, are wary of honoring a general power of attorney and want you to fill out their particular form. If you can't come to the bank, perhaps a notary can come to your house with the bank form.

A power of attorney requires two notarized signatures, the grantor's and the agent's. This is one way the law protects the grantor against abuses.

In 2009, in order to curb abuses of agents compensating themselves or just plain stealing money, the one page Power of Attorney form morphed into six pages complete with warnings and instructions similar to "thou shall not steal."

A power of attorney can be revoked by the grantor at any time. I advise my clients to protect themselves by writing letters to their agent and to all their financial institutions that they have revoked their POA and also to put real estate firms on notice.

All in all, the power of attorney is a very useful document that keeps your financial transactions from grinding to a halt when you are indisposed or unavailable. Care must be taken that the agent is trustworthy and that the document is not given to the agent until the principal is unable to act on his or her own. It is always better to have it and not use it than to need it when it's already too late.

Your attorney should be consulted to ensure your POA is properly executed.

A will, a living will, a health care proxy and a power of attorney–when you have them all, you can relax–knowing you've gotten a *Clean Bill of Legal Health!*

Robert Howe may be reached at 718 748 9700 or rhowe@robert-howe.com"

"Robert Howe shares his over 36 years of legal experience consulting with Seniors on how to organize their legal life in order to enjoy their personal life. His most satisfying moments are when a client tells him years later, "your advice was perfect, I left your office knowing I was in good hands".

REVERSE
MORE FORWARD WE GO MORE BEHIND WE GET
LET'S MOVE FORWARD IN REVERSE
MØRTGAGE

MOVING FORWARD IN REVERSE

Most of you have seen the commercials– Robert Wagner, the dashing star of movies and television, invites you to order a DVD about reverse mortgages. Though the ads may be intriguing, some seniors have been dissuaded from looking into reverse mortgages by all the myths attached to them– including the myth that once you take out a reverse mortgage, the bank owns your house.

Hello, I'm Annette Fisher, Senior Advisor, and Reverse Mortgage Loan Originator, at Fort Funding Corp. Over the years I have heard many wonderful stories from the families of our borrowers. A FHA reverse mortgage, also known as a HECM, Home Equity Conversion Mortgage was created in the 1980s to make it possible for seniors to afford living in their homes with dignity and independence. It allows homeowners 62 and over to tap into the equity that has been stashed away in their houses.

The best part of a reverse mortgage is you never have to make monthly payments, of principal and interest. When a homeowner borrows against his house with a reverse mortgage, the bank pays you, or perhaps pays off an existing mortgage! The homeowner can either take out a lump sum, a line of credit, monthly tenure payments (payments for life), monthly term payments or a combination of payments.

A reverse mortgage is considered borrowed money, so it will not affect your social security. Homeowners using a reverse mortgage must pay their property taxes, home-owners' insurance, keep up with basic repairs, and live in the home as their primary residence.

Another terrific feature of a reverse mortgage is that you do not have to give up ownership of your home. Repayment of the mortgage balance is not due until the last of the borrowers is no longer living in the home. If a person dies or decides to sell their home – and yes, you have the right to sell your home without asking the lender's permission– the reverse mortgage is first satisfied, and then the remaining proceeds go to you or your estate. Unlike traditional mortgages the borrower is not the one securing the debt, it is secured by the property. In July of 2011, a new ruling established that if the borrower owes more than the current value of the home, the heirs, or whoever is purchasing the home could pay 95% of the current value of the home to extinguish the debt. The servicing department must agree to the value derived by the appraiser. Whoever is requesting the update to the current value on the property usually pays for that appraisal. In the past if someone from the family was purchasing a family home that had a reverse mortgage, HUD would require that the debt be paid in full, regardless of the current value. Also in August of 2014 a HUD mortgagee letter was distributed stating if a none borrowing spouse who was married to the borrower, living in the home at the time of application and the application was done after August 14,2014 then that person could continue to live in the home even if the last remaining borrower had passed. However if there is an open line of credit it would have been frozen upon the notification of the death of the last remaining borrower.

After nearly 12 years working with seniors as a loan originator and or a reverse mortgage processor, I have seen how this financial vehicle has improved the overall quality of people's lives, from lifting them out of poverty to simply giving them more joy. Life is for living, and struggling to barely keep a roof over your head is not enough. It is important to understand how reverse mortgages can be used by you or loved ones to maximum benefit; each situation is unique. The following examples will help you debunk the myths, learn the basics and figure out the right questions to ask when seeking a reverse mortgage.

Mr. Bee was a very good natured middle-aged man who was very bad at finances. He came to me genuinely upset, fearing his situation was hopeless. His mom, Mary, and Aunt Joanne had deeded him the home they'd lived in for over forty years because they felt it was the best way to make sure he inherited it. The home was now in foreclosure. Mr. Bee had taken out a mortgage on the house and in just a few years had used up all the money to do some remodeling, buy a car, pay off his credit cards and enjoy life. He had tried to do a loan modification; however, he couldn't justify hardship to the lender. And to make matters worse, since Mr. Bee wasn't living in the house, the family home of four decades that his mother and aunt still occupied was disqualified and treated as an investment property in regard to a mortgage modification. Mr. Bee was in his mid-40's so he wasn't old enough to do a reverse mortgage. He was more than willing to give the home back to his mom and aunt so they could do one. But to his surprise, several loan officers he spoke to told him that his elderly aunt and mother couldn't immediately obtain a reverse mortgage because of the recently enacted "seasoning" rule.

In 2007, when the housing and banking crisis hit, some homeowners younger than 62 started avoiding making monthly mortgage payments by deeding their homes to senior relatives who could be persuaded to move in with them; then the seniors would take out a reverse mortgage on the home.

To stop this, the FHA passed a rule, with this basic guideline; when a property is transferred between family members, the deed must be "seasoned" for 12 months before a reverse mortgage can be done.

Loan officers hearing Mr. Bee's story simply applied pro forma this seasoning rule to say that his aunt and mother had to have the deed in their names for 12 months before they could get a reverse mortgage. So his aunt and mother were out of luck and out of their home; they would lose it to foreclosure before it could be saved.

On their social security alone, these ladies could not even have afforded to rent an apartment. After listening to Mr. Bee's story, I asked Mr. Bee if his mom and aunt were still living in the house and if they'd ever moved out for any period of time. I was encouraged to hear they had lived there continually for forty years. I asked the ladies to send us utility bills for the last year. They gathered their utility bills and other documents proving they had never stopped living in their home. The bank Underwriter agreed that the house had truly always been these two seniors' primary home. So the 12-month seasoning rule was waived. In the end Mr. Bee deeded the family home back to his mom and aunt, and they are still living there stress free, and collecting rent from the two apartments and the store that are part of the building with their primary residence.

The above example is also important because it illustrates an important distinction, especially in these tough economic times, between a traditional mortgage and a reverse mortgage. As I mentioned, the two seniors Mary and Joanne did not have enough money to rent an apartment even if they pooled their social security. This meant of course they could never have qualified for any home equity line of credit or a second mortgage on the house. The only other road for them to have taken would have been to sell. Since the building was a four unit dwelling, their accountant indicated a lot of taxes would be due, and rent would cost much more than their overhead at the time.

The biggest benefit of a reverse mortgage is, no monthly payments of principal and interest are required for as long as the borrower remains in the home as their primary residence and continues to keep up with real estate taxes, property insurance and basic upkeep of the home. In addition the loan CAN NOT be rescinded by the lender just because they feel like they no longer want the risk on their books. Even if the funds from the reverse mortgage run out you can still remain in the home.

Many changes took place on October 1, 2013 limiting the amount of principal that can be released and an Asset test much like a debt to income ratio was set to go into effect on January 13, 2014. Although HUD, Housing & Urban Development has held off on implementing the January 13th Asset Test, they have now implemented the Asset Test as of April 27th, 2015. To understand the October 1, 2013 ruling (60% rule), it is best to have a discussion with a licensed Loan Originator/Officer who is highly knowledgeable in the area of reverse mortgages. Although many Loan Originators will tell you they can help you with a reverse mortgage, they may not know the programs well. Therefore, they send you a proposal because any Loan Originator can print one out. However, some have no clue how reverse mortgages work in relation to living trusts, irrevocable trusts, pooled trusts, Medicaid, or a Life Estate. Since I have been helping seniors in this area for over a decade, and have worked side by side with many attorneys in NY and NJ, and most of my referrals come from Estate Planning Attorneys and Financial Planners, I'm very knowledgeable in this area; therefore I know the right questions to ask. I always want to involve you, your family and other advisers to get the best possible solution for you.

Be aware, the rules for FHA HECM mortgages are subject to change. In recent years it has been harder and harder for seniors to make ends meet–the value in some cases of their homes and portfolios have plummeted, they can barely earn any interest at the bank, and some have been watching their retirement funds not just dwindle but disappear. The banks have tightened up credit and seniors who once assumed they could safely secure lines of credit, are not qualifying.

Even more distressing, back in 2008 when the banks began their meltdown, many decided to call-in the lines of credit they had issued. In a reverse mortgage, the funds are guaranteed for as long as you live in the home, pay the homeowners insurance, real estate taxes and basic upkeep of the home. In other words, if you decide to take out a line of credit on a FHA reverse mortgage you never have to worry that it will be called in.

I have worked with several of our clients who saw reverse mortgages as their only salvation from outliving their retirement funds. The Clarks were a good example of a couple that could no longer count on the traditional mortgage market. They came to me a couple of years ago frantic because they had taken out a home equity loan nearly 15 years before, and had just received a letter from the bank saying their home equity line was coming due. They were expected to make a balloon payment of $150, 000. They were both retired at this point and had other bills, such as credit cards, and car payments every month. The reverse mortgage was a real lifesaver because they would not have qualified for a conventional mortgage. Even better, they no longer had to make that monthly payment to their old home equity loan.

We once had to disappoint a woman, Mildred who called from Florida about getting a reverse mortgage on her condominium; she had just buried her husband days before. She explained, the bank had just informed her that the home equity line of credit on her condo was no longer available. Mildred wanted to do a reverse mortgage; however, this was not her primary residence, which was a rent-controlled apartment in NYC. She eventually sold the condo since giving up her rent controlled NYC apartment was out of the question.

The one absolute requirement for obtaining a HECM reverse mortgage on a home is that it must be your primary residence. You must file your taxes at that address, receive your social security award letter there, and it must be the listed address on your driving license or non driving government ID card. You can go on long vacations–up to one year. You can even have a vacation home.

As long as you aren't gone from your home for more than the 12 months, you're in compliance. Furthermore, lenders send periodic notices to the primary residence, which the homeowner is expected to fill out and return. If these notices are repeatedly ignored, that will send up a red flag to the lender that the resident might not be using this as a primary home. This requirement can be difficult for seniors, who sometimes don't go through their mail carefully enough and are quick to pile up all mail as junk.

The house also cannot be rented out for a portion of the year by the homeowner, though a reverse mortgage can be done on a 1-4 family home and the other apartments in the multi-family home can be rented. Although the FHA does allow a reverse mortgage to be done on mixed-use properties, the commercial portion of the property currently must be less than 25 percent of the usable area of the building. In addition, a property can be refused based on the type of commercial occupancy. This is decided on a case-by-case basis. Lenders are much more likely to approve a business that is run by the homeowner than an outsider, and one that doesn't bring in a lot of outside traffic. It is however always up to the discretion of the underwriter.

Two other senior sisters, Betty and Paula, we dealt with had a problem not just because of the commercial use of their property but also because they didn't even seem to own the property at all.

In a period of a week I received calls from several people regarding Betty and Paula, who were about to lose their three million-dollar family home. A loan officer warned me I was wasting my time because these ladies didn't even own the property. The sisters had inherited the home from their parents free and clear. Betty was a widow. Unbeknownst to both Betty and Paula, two trusting souls who didn't understand much about finances, their sister-in-law had stolen their house from them. How can someone steal a house? You can't exactly put it in your pocket or grab it at gunpoint. Since Betty and Paula didn't have a mortgage on the house, the sister-in-law simply faked a deed and recorded it at the courthouse. The first they learned of it, Betty and Paula told me, was when they received a notice taped to their front door that the house would be auctioned off in 30 days for failure to pay real estate taxes. They had never paid any tax bills because they believed their sister-in-law was taking care of it!

I told them they needed an attorney immediately to get the deed vacated that the sister-in-law had forged. I also told them they needed to find money immediately to pay off the tax lien, which was $20,000. Since they had no funds, I suggested the sisters work with an attorney to find private investors willing to loan them the money. Of course, it would take some convincing to get an investor since the ladies had no collateral. They did get the funds to pay off the tax lien and avoid the auction! It took an entire year and many thousands of dollars in legal fees to get the deed vacated. After finally getting the house back in their name, they took out a traditional mortgage to make some much-needed repairs and pay back the high-interest short-term loan. They had wanted to do a reverse mortgage but at the time, they were renting out a portion of their home as a doctor's office, and the business was not given approval by the Underwriter. After a couple of years paying a conventional mortgage, the women were strapped for cash. The lease on the doctor's office was up, and they realized it made much more financial sense to stop renting out the office. Finally, they were able to get a reverse mortgage, and they were free of monthly mortgage payments.

So far, we have been addressing who qualifies for a reverse mortgage (a senior who's the primary homeowner) and the type of property. Nevertheless, the next question becomes, how much? How much money will a reverse mortgage allow you to take out of your property? In addition, what are the costs associated with taking out the reverse mortgage? As with all aspects of a reverse mortgage, it depends.

The older you are and the more equity you have in your house, the larger the amount of principal allowed to be borrowed with a HECM reverse mortgage. Moreover, your choice of how you receive your money affects how much money is available to you. Remember you have options: You can receive a lump sum payment up front, up to the limit available. You can get monthly tenure payments, which are life payments (well, technically payments until you're 150 years old–but so far none of our clients has outlived their payments!). Alternatively, if you want your monthly payments to be larger– you can get term limits–for example 10 years. Furthermore, in some cases, you can get an equity line of credit that you tap into only when you decide to. So, ask to have a loan officer give you examples of the various reverse mortgage programs that are available.

Again, the beauty of a reverse mortgage is that it is flexible enough to suit most needs. You can start off getting tenure payments, but if unfortunately you have a stroke or become terminally ill and suddenly need expensive round the clock care, you can convert your payments to a term limit and use the possibly larger monthly checks to pay for nurses, home aides etc. and hopefully avoid a nursing home. As of Oct. 1, 2013 you can take up to 60% of the principal made available in the first year, minus closing costs or more if there are mandatory obligations to be paid off. You can also pull out up to 10% cash above the mandatory obligations that exceed the 60%, if it is available in the principle limit. The non-recourse insurance upfront premium is based on the initial percentage released. If you do not need to tap into more than 60% of the principal limit available including the cost to close the loan you can see a substantial savings on the premium, in many cases thousands of dollars.

When it comes to determining the amount of equity you can pull out of your house, federal guidelines determine the maximum. During the past few years, one of the rare pieces of good news in the mortgage lending sector occurred in 2009, when the FHA standardized and raised the maximum claim amount to $625,500 for reverse mortgages nationwide (with the exception of a few states where it's even higher). Prior to this, the maximum amount of home value taken into consideration for a home owner to borrow against for purposes of a reverse mortgage varied not just from state to state, but even from county to county, with some counties capping it at as little as $200,000 to $417,000. So, if your house had $700,000 value prior to 2009, the program would only recognize a maximum of $417,000 of property value and in some counties less. Now if your home is valued at $700,000, in almost all 50 states, a value of $625,500 will be recognized when calculating how large a reverse mortgage you are entitled to, and in the remaining states it will be more! 2017 Nationwide HECM Loan Limit Increase. FHA recently published Mortgagee Letter 2016-19, which provides the 2017 maximum (max) claim amount for HECM loans. The max claim amount (also known as the lending limit) has increased to $636,150. These limits are applicable for case numbers assigned on or after January 1, 2017

Typically, you can get a reverse mortgage for about 50 to 75 percent of the lower of the maximum claim amount or the appraised value of your home. However, as of October 1, 2013 you may not be able to touch a percentage of the funding for twelve months. It is not true that you have to own your home outright. One of the criteria for a reverse mortgage is you must have enough equity in your home, or you can bring money to closing to pay your original mortgage off. It is true that to receive a reverse mortgage, you must pay off all other liens, home equity lines of credit, mortgages, or loans against the property. Nevertheless, the beauty of the program is you can use some of the proceeds from your reverse mortgage to pay off these encumbrances at closing. Moreover, you can pay off most of the closing costs and fees associated with the loan by wrapping them into your reverse mortgage.

A cost unique to reverse mortgages is mandatory "non-recourse" insurance. This insurance limits the liability for the reverse mortgage to the value of the property or the balance owed to the lender whichever is lower. If an immediate family member wished to purchase the home, prior to July 2011, and more was owed to the lender than the value of the home, that purchaser would have had to pay the true balance regardless of the home's value. Now non-recourse insurance reduces the primary max purchase price, for primary family members, to keep the home when all borrowers have passed to 95% of the value of the home. When you sell your home, or die, you or your estate must repay the funds you received from the reverse mortgage plus interest and other fees, to the lender. Non-recourse insurance can be expensive: it is based on the maximum claim amount or the appraised value, whichever is lower for the upfront premium as previously mentioned, plus an additional percentage every year, of the total outstanding reverse mortgage balance, as set by FHA, Federal Housing Administration. Most important Non-Recourse insurance prevents reverse mortgage debt being attached to anyone. HECM debt, unlike conventional mortgages, is only linked to the house.

In order to reduce the high closing costs on reverse mortgages, the FHA had implemented a program known as a HECM Saver a few years ago. That program had reduced the cost for the mandatory non-recourse insurance in many cases by thousands of dollars. In some cases, the savings was $10,000 to $12,000. However, there was a trade-off; it had reduced the percentage of funds a senior was able to borrow against the property. Therefore, the new method of taking less than 60% of the principal for a lower upfront premium is similar to how the saver program worked, in that it can save you thousands of dollars on the cost of closing your reverse mortgage.

As with most mortgages, you are charged interest, the amount of which is dependent on what rates are available at the time and whether you get a fixed or variable rate. And you are charged only for the amount of money you've actually borrowed, so that if you barely tap into a line of credit or sell the house after receiving only a few monthly payments, you only pay back those sums plus fees, and interest. Every month you should get a statement from the lender telling you how much you or your estate will owe, at that moment in time.

In areas where the home values had fallen substantially, seniors unfortunately have suffered because some no longer have enough equity for a reverse mortgage. However, it is important to challenge an assessment if your home falls short.

In recent years home values have started to climb back up, so if you were told you did not have enough equity to qualify a few years ago, 2008-2015, you might have enough equity to qualify at this point. You also are now older which allows for a higher percentage of funds to be available. Also additional payments you had made may have increased your equity.

Many folks who are very well off financially are starting to see some of the benefits in doing a reverse mortgage, like possibly reducing estate taxes later on by reducing the value of your estate now. Folks save what they think is plenty for retirement, however do they have any insurance against estate taxes? Although the purchasing of these policies for this purpose would not make sense for the person who barely has enough money to get by; I have heard many insurance agents speak about getting insurance to protect against estate taxes. Insurance purchased when a person is a senior can be very expensive, you should check with a licensed insurance agent, your accountant, and an estate-planning attorney if you think such a solution could help preserve the wealth of your family's estate.

For years, Miss Argold had taken care of foster kids, but she was slowing down, and her grown son, who helped pay the bills, was moving out. Even though Miss Argold came to us for a reverse mortgage, she worried she would not qualify. She told me that although her house had been worth $500,000 the year before, it was now only worth $350,000. Even considering the 2008 housing crisis, I was surprised that the value of a home in the five boroughs of New York would have dropped over 33 percent in one year. When I asked her why she thought the house was only worth $350,000, she told me that other reverse mortgage consultants had mentioned the two foreclosures on her block. I immediately called an appraiser, who told me that unless the majority of homes in an area are being foreclosed, the foreclosure sale prices are thrown out because they are not necessarily indicative of an entire neighborhood. Miss Argold closed on her reverse mortgage with a value of $475,000.

The fallout from the housing crisis has reverberated in other ways. Because Lehman Brothers was the only investor of coop and jumbo reverse mortgages, these are –at least for now–no longer available. And rules tightening condo reverse mortgages make them sometimes more difficult and costly for most of New York City condos, since a condo association must now be pre-approved by

FHA (which might be costly, if the management has to pay a management company or expert in the area to prepare a package for FHA approval).

On a positive note, the housing crisis has spurred the banking department to toughen up the rules for the industry as a whole.

As a first step to receiving a reverse mortgage, all borrowers are required to be counseled by an HUD approved agency. Counselors not only cover information regarding reverse mortgages, they also go through a budget with the borrower. Counselors may also make suggestions regarding various programs that are available to borrowers in addition to a reverse mortgage. Sometimes heat, roofing or window repair assistance is available. Many neighborhoods also have food programs available. The primary job of the counseling agency is to make sure seniors are not being taken advantage of. Counseling can be done over the phone or in person. The loan originator provides a list of counselors; however, a big red flag should go up if a loan originator suggests a particular counselor and/or offers to call the counselor for you.

In addition, seniors receiving benefits from special assistance programs should always consult the program director. Under some programs, funds from a reverse mortgage may be considered assets that disqualify a senior. Sometimes an Estate Planning Attorney can set up a pooled trust to have reverse mortgage funds pay for your necessities of daily living, and in many situations still allow you to qualify for aid from other programs.

There are no limitations as to what a reverse mortgage can do for you. Just let your imagination run wild. Many of our clients have used the funds from their reverse mortgage to buy retirement homes in a bad market with a lower price tag, while waiting for the market to turn around and sell their primary residence in a better market.

Reverse mortgages can even be used to purchase a primary residence. A reverse mortgage purchase requires a larger down payment and is usually used in situations where the borrower sold their prior residence. Moreover, this allows the borrower to live without monthly mortgage payments of principal and interest, and may make some of the funds available from the previous sale for the homeowner to use on something else.

As I have said, the reverse mortgage opens up all sorts of possibilities. For many of our clients, the most rewarding part of getting a reverse mortgage has been the ability to help their families while they were still alive; some have even helped their grandchildren to buy homes. For these seniors and for so many others we have worked with, a reverse mortgage has not just been valuable but priceless. For those folks wishing to make monthly payments in order to keep the balance from accruing (higher interest) and using up equity, the good news is there are no prepayment penalties. In addition, if at some point you choose to stop making monthly payments you can do so at any time. Keep in mind; you do need to be at least 62 to get approval for an FHA reverse mortgage.

However it is possible to remove a younger borrower in order to qualify and if that younger borrower is the spouse of the borrower they would still have some protection under the rules set forth in the August 2014 mortgagee letter.

Sometimes borrowers will use a reverse mortgage in a way that is similar to an insurance policy. You can take out a reverse mortgage as a full line of credit. The good news with a line of credit is, the credit line grows according to the average interest rate on the product at the time plus the cost of the percentage for FHA insurance. What this means for the borrower is the credit line will continue to grow to keep up with inflation. This is an excellent back up plan when there are two incomes and you may be wondering how the remaining person will make ends meet when the other person's income may no longer be available. Also it is easier to set up the reverse mortgage when all parties are competent.

Even with a power of attorney, POA, a borrower's designated agent for POA may have challenges when trying to do a reverse mortgage. This is because if the POA is being used because someone is incompetent, then the underwriter will want a letter indicating the other borrower is incompetent. This is not always as easy as it may seem to obtain.

Some doctors do not want to issue these letters because if a financial impropriety occurs, they do not want to have responsibility for the impropriety. Should this be the situation all hope of obtaining a reverse mortgage may not be exhausted. There is still the possibility of obtaining a court ordered guardianship. Many times in such a case the courts will appoint someone to audit the use of the monies distributed by the guardian.

In some cases where a borrower/s does not qualify, the answer is to sell the home. In many cases, a home of lesser value might be the answer. Again, this might be a situation where a borrower may choose to sell the home and then do a reverse purchase as long as the next home is a one family or pre FHA approved Condominium. Although the reverse mortgage HECM product is technically available up to a 4 family, I have not found a lender who will approve a HECM reverse purchase on a 2-4 family/unit building. Perhaps homecare is the reason the funds from a reverse seemed like the solution, yet it didn't work out because of lending limits. Maybe selling the home and perhaps an assisted living residence is the answer. For each person that I speak with, the picture seems to be a little different. There really is no one size fits all answer when it comes to people. The point is, when you are making plans and it involves your home, you do not need to do it all alone; I am here to help if you just want to pick up the phone.

For a complimentary initial consultation, and a free reverse mortgage kit, please call, Annette on her cell phone at

347-291-7479. Annette Fisher, Reverse Mortgage Loan Originator, NMLS 67606 *Licensed in NY and NJ for Reverse, Residential and Commercial Mortgages.*

Fort Funding Corp. NMLS 39463, toll free 877-228-4404 Licensed by New Jersey Department of Banking and Insurance, Registered Mortgage Broker New York State Department of Financial Services. Loans Arranged Through Third Party lenders. Connecticut Mortgage Broker Only, Not a Lender or Mortgage Correspondent Lender. Equal Housing Opportunity. Corporate office: 7016 Fort Hamilton Parkway, Brooklyn NY 11228 🏠

Annette Fisher, NY State Approved Technical Instructor for Mortgage and Lending Practices Real Estate Course. Licensed Real Estate Agent, 347-291-7479 BRESRE Realty 3735 Oceanic Avenue Brooklyn NY 11224. 718-513-6002

HOME CARE, HOME IS WHERE THE HEART IS

A Scary Start to the Day

It was frightening to see! She was lying on the floor in the kitchen, trying to act calm but clearly scared. She had fallen trying to fix herself breakfast. We did a quick check to see if she was hurt, brushed off the toast crumbs on her nightgown and helped her up. Thank goodness, she had not broken any bones. This was our first encounter with Mrs. Marcu

Unfortunately, the story of Mrs. Marcu reflects a common problem in our country. A 1997 survey done by the National Alliance for Caregiving and AARP, and updated in 2004, found that in an estimated 22.9 million U.S. households, there is someone who can not manage alone and needs the care provided by a friend, relative or an outside companion.

It's hard to imagine that so many families in America have the additional responsibility of caring for an older relative. We, the baby boomers, born between 1946 and 1965, are a generation of adults who must deal with the stress of juggling children, careers, as well as caring for our parents.

Moreover, the role we find ourselves least prepared for, the one that tugs at our hearts, is caring for our parents.

The very people who cared for us, the ones who guided us throughout our lives, now need our help! Moreover, we want to make sure they are safe and looked after as best we can.

I'm Marie Sayour, and our company, RN Staffing Solutions, LLC, was created because we recognized the need for quality home caregivers for seniors in the New York City area when friends and relatives approached us time and again asking for our assistance. They weren't asking for us to come into a loved ones home to provide medical services. Rather what these families wanted--what they really required–were reliable, compassionate caregivers who were trained to assist elderly relatives with their daily lives.

Our philosophy is that sending a caregiver into your loved one's home should not mean just sending in a warm body. Our company is dedicated to matching the right caregiver with the right senior so that our employee will fit into the senior's household, providing not just needed services, but adding pleasure to a senior's day. As such, we consider it important to not only screen and train our companions but also to carefully interview our seniors to understand their needs.

We find out the list of medications seniors use and their medical conditions. We inspect the environment they live in to make sure there are no booby traps–a seemingly innocuous item such as a scatter rug can be an accident waiting to happen for a senior who is unsteady on his feet.

We want to be prepared – we take emergency contact info. If a person lives alone the majority of the time, we might suggest a life alert or another emergency system they can use to get help. Though most of our caregivers don't usually stay full-time at a senior's home, we are flexible with our schedules and can also provide "live-in" services.

And two out of three of our managing partners are nurses. Though we provide non-medical caregivers, we often times send a nurse to evaluate a senior at home as part of our initial assessment to see what a senior requires. This proved to be a life-saving strategy on at least one occasion.

Staying Alive

One night after business hours, we received a phone call from a woman who was concerned about her elderly neighbor because she'd noticed some changes in her friend over the last few days. Initially the woman simply mentioned on the phone that she thought her neighbor would benefit from a companion. We were about to schedule an appointment for the next morning to visit and assess the senior. But there was some urgency in this woman's voice that made us heed her plea to visit that very night.

When we met Maura, she was sitting on the couch with a smile on her face. Her neighbor, however, did not have the same calm demeanor. It was not until we offered to walk Maura to the bathroom that alarm bells went off in our heads. Maura was completely unsteady and walked with a peculiar gait. Her neighbor, deeply concerned, explained that Maura did not usually walk this way. Not only that, she said that Maura's speech and tone were strange. "This is not how Maura sounds. This is not how she walks," the neighbor said.

In other words, there was something drastically wrong. Since Maura's children lived out of state, the neighbor was the one to keep in touch with the family if there were any problems. We told the neighbor that Maura needed immediate medical attention, and we called 911.

We were able to have one of our caregivers escort a frightened Maura in the ambulance. She was admitted to the hospital, where it was found that she had a bleed on the brain, and she was rushed to surgery. After spending time in the ICU, Maura was transferred to a rehabilitation facility where she made a remarkable recovery.

Today, Maura is fine. She's back to an active social life, going out to dinner and the theater with friends. She has worked hard to relearn to walk with the use of a walker or cane. She is even considering driving again.

In Maura's case, the service we offered, unexpectedly, was to get her immediate life saving medical attention. But in most cases, what we do is find the right companion to meet the physical and emotional needs of mom and dad. Maybe it will brighten mom's day if her caregiver takes her to get her hair done at her favorite beauty salon or drives her to a favorite store. Sometimes just having someone visit with mom or dad wards off her sense of loneliness and depression. And of course, there are many ways that a senior needs help around the house–it can make a big difference in a senior's life if someone comes in the morning to cook them breakfast and help them get dressed, does some light housekeeping and tidying up – all the things a senior might not be able to do anymore by themselves.

Often our clients are coming out of rehab and making their transition back home. It gives them and/or their family a sense of security to have someone in place every day to make sure they get their meals and are safe doing daily activities such as showering.

But there are a myriad of ways that a companion can make a difference; even such things as escorting a senior to a wedding so she can have some help going to the ladies room.

One of the most important aspects of our services is that it is often an alternative to the unwanted decision to place mom or dad in a nursing home. We enable seniors to stay in their homes and live more independent fulfilled lives.

We train and screen our caregivers to make sure your relative isn't just with someone reliable but with someone nice. It is important to hire caregivers who are kindhearted and treat clients with respect and dignity.

This chapter highlights some of the real life situations we have been called in to help with, as well as offers additional information on caring for senior relatives living at home. One of the purposes of this chapter is to demonstrate that as a senior, you are not alone and there is help available, no matter what the situation might be.

Finding Her Way Home

Molly is an 89-year-old woman who has lived in her apartment building most of her adult life. She knew her neighborhood well and loved walking to the avenue to shop or get her hair done at her favorite beauty salon. But recently, on several occasions neighbors would find her wandering around the neighborhood, unable to remember how to get back to her apartment.

Molly was lucky that her kind neighbors escorted her home. Molly has no family living nearby. She has only a granddaughter who lives far from New York City.

Her granddaughter actually picked up subtle changes in Molly's mental status when she talked to her on the phone and noticed that her grandmother was not responding appropriately to conversations. Worried about her, the granddaughter came to visit, and while here, she contacted us for a consultation.

When we met Molly, she was gracious, charming, and quite adept at disguising her confusion. She had an easy time remembering events and people in her life but her short-term memory was weak.

We placed a compassionate caregiver with Molly so that she could remain comfortable and still safe in her own home. Her granddaughter was greatly relieved that there was someone watching out for her grandmother on a daily basis. The caregiver has also been able to monitor Molly's progress and report on her deterioration, so that her granddaughter will be able to judge when Molly is no longer able to be cared for at home.

According to the National Institute on Aging, Alzheimer's is a progressive brain disease that slowly destroys memory and reasoning skills and eventually even the ability to carry out the simplest tasks. In most people with Alzheimer's, symptoms first appear after age 60. Experts estimate that as many as 5.1 million Americans may have Alzheimer's.

Memory loss and its most extreme form, dementia, are common health problems among the elderly in the United States. Dementia is the loss of cognitive functioning—thinking, remembering, and reasoning— to such an extent that it interferes with a person's daily life and activities. There are various causes of dementia, with Alzheimer's disease the most common cause among older people.

Memory problems are one of the first signs of Alzheimer's. There are different phases of Alzheimer's disease from mild to severe, and it is not yet fully understood. There are certain early signs and/or symptoms that a loved one is developing Alzheimer's such as:

1. Communication is hard for people with Alzheimer disease. They may struggle to find words or forget what they want to say. They may have problems understanding a conversation or paying attention during one. A senior may even start regularly responding to questions that weren't asked.
2. They experience frequent falls for no reason.
3. They forget to turn off the stove.
4. They stop paying bills.
5. They might put cash in the mail to pay for something or even fall prey to obvious money scams.
6. They have trouble recognizing a close loved one or inappropriately greet a total stranger.
7. They keep asking where they are, when it should be obvious.
8. They forget how to use such ordinary items as the telephone, or the microwave; they forget how to cook or turn on the faucet, or to button an article of clothing.
9. They wear the same clothes day after day, forget to bathe or stop caring about their appearance.

You may notice personality changes in the individual. They might become more easily upset, worried or angry.

They might be depressed. They might hide things or think that people are hiding things from them.

Though we don't know the cause of AD (except in a very small percentage of early onset cases caused by a genetic mutation), there are some things we can do to help ourselves and our parents stay mentally sharp. Keep cholesterol and blood pressure under control. Eat healthy, exercise, don't smoke, or drink alcohol to excess. Stimulate your brain. Challenge it with mind games or other activities that will require your brain to work. Keep socially active; studies have shown that people with active social lives have a slower rate of memory decline.

Giving A Norwegian Gem Back Her Luster

It all started with a fall and an ambulance ride to the hospital. One summer day, while out for a walk, Hilda a 93-year-old vivacious woman, tripped over a tree trunk and fell hard on her face. A kind stranger who saw her lying on the ground with blood gushing from her face called 911. This event alarmed her granddaughter, who flew in from out West to help sort things out.

Hilda is a lively woman who led a privileged life as a child raised on a farm in Norway. An intelligent woman, she studied hard and became a nurse. She left her family and immigrated to the United States.

She worked in a Manhattan hospital and met the man she would marry. She lived for many years in a luxury apartment on prestigious Fifth Avenue. She and her husband eventually moved to Brooklyn, where she lives to this day alone (her husband passed away some years ago).

Hilda is very worldly and has always been known to read *The New York Times* from beginning to end everyday. She converses about all current events from the latest on Tiger Woods (she's an avid fan!) to the current political climate.

However, her granddaughter noticed that Hilda didn't seem as sharp as she had been. A series of medical tests ruled out any brain injury from the fall. The granddaughter was concerned that the change in Hilda's mental status was perhaps the beginning of Alzheimer's.

But one of the observations made by the granddaughter was that Hilda was not eating well. It turned out that Hilda was forgetting to eat, and in general finding it a bit overwhelming to continue preparing meals for herself.

We were asked to provide a caregiver seven days a week, twice a day, primarily to insure that Hilda was given nutritious meals. Within a few weeks of our working with Hilda, she blossomed. The change in her was overwhelming!! She was back to her old self. Her color had returned to her cheeks, her strength and stamina had improved, and she was as chatty as ever with all of us who visited. It was so wonderful to see.

Her doctor arranged to have a physical therapist come to her house to help her regain her balance and stability with the use of a walker, which she now refers to as "her best friend."

The caregivers assigned to her have become more than just professional acquaintances. Hilda has become 'adopted' as an honorary elder and is known to give advice to the caregivers on a regular basis!

We provide a caregiver in the morning to help her with grooming, hygiene and breakfast, and someone in the evening for dinner preparation and turn down service. We also take care of her laundry, grocery shopping and escort Hilda to the beauty shop and physician appointments.

The nutritional needs of seniors are unlike that of any other age group. As we age, our metabolism slows down. And our bodies don't absorb needed nutrients as successfully as when we were younger. So, proper nutrition for Hilda is vital for her health.

In addition, seniors often eat alone, and there is a correlation between living alone and having poorer quality diets. Seniors, who become isolated, depressed or lonely, might not feel like eating. Sometimes, they forget to eat. Some with emotional issues may overeat.

Some seniors have medical problems that interfere with their ability to eat. Difficulty chewing or swallowing, difficultly with digestion, or even a loss of appetite can prevent seniors from consuming their meals.

But a healthy diet is of paramount importance. Constipation, diabetes, high blood pressure, high cholesterol, and malnutrition – these are all just some of the serious medical problems related to poor diet.

Some of the lesser known telltale signs that a loved one isn't getting adequate nutrition is that she has a lot of bruises or a gray skin color, lacks energy or even, as in Hilda's case, appears confused.

Fortunately, there are options. For someone like Hilda, the best solution was hiring a caregiver who can shop for her and prepare meals. On the other hand, you can arrange to have meals delivered to you. This eliminates the need for grocery shopping and meal preparation. Programs like Meals on Wheels deliver meals several times a week to seniors who have financial constraints.

And remember, dining alone should be made a pleasurable experience. Just set the table at your favorite eating spot and enjoy! And make sure that your diet includes high fiber foods, such as fruits and vegetables. Drink plenty of water. Keep your calcium, Vitamin D and B12 levels within normal limits. Eat foods high in protein unless you are on a restricted diet where your doctor has advised you otherwise.

Eat healthy and have a healthy life. This is a good goal for all of us. If we make the necessary changes in our diets gradually, we can create habits and a lifestyle that will add productive years to our lives.

Caregivers should be sensitive to the tastes of a senior. We ask our clients how they prefer to have their meals prepared, which ingredients, etc. If we are placing a caregiver in a home where they are required to cook, we make sure they are capable of preparing foods that the senior enjoys eating.

This is all part of our dedication to making sure that our caregivers are the right fit for the senior they're assisting. Aside from standard criminal background checks and calling professional references, we provide orientations explaining exactly how a caregiver should handle different situations such as dealing with someone with dementia, a person who can't dress themselves or a person who feels lonely.

We ask a myriad of questions that go beyond just finding out if a potential caregiver is competent. For example, do they like cats and/or dogs? Are they allergic? We don't want to place a caregiver who doesn't like pets in the home of a senior who is dearly attached to her dog. Our goal is always to find the caregiver who can blend right into a client's household and foster a caring relationship with that senior.

Loneliness Shouldn't Be Your Only Companion in Old Age

Connie is 4ft. 8in. with shoes on. Short, but what a sweet woman! Speaking first with her on the phone to get some information, I imagined her to be a young, strong woman who was calling for an older family member. I was taken aback when she told me she was 93-years-old and was inquiring for herself! Connie was sharp as a tack and was managing most of her daily chores just fine. The reason for the call–Connie was lonely.

The only living family member she had left was a brother who lived out of town and offered to pay for someone to come to her home a few times a week to keep Connie company. We matched her up with a lovely young woman who was able to help Connie do some things that were becoming a bit difficult for her, such as food shopping, cleaning her apartment and cooking some meals.

One of the most touching comments I remember Connie saying came after one weekend in particular: "We (the caregiver and Connie) shared a meal. We were just like family!"

Connie has thrived as a result of the companionship and conversation. And we improvised to make our caregiver as accessible to Connie as possible. Connie is extremely hard of hearing and wears a hearing aide. So she often doesn't hear the caregiver knocking on her door. We came up with a system to announce the caregiver's arrival. The caregiver calls me, I call Connie (who can hear the phone more easily than the front door), and Connie lets the caregiver in.

Things are getting better now that we are on a consistent schedule, and Connie waits for the knock now. It was funny for a while though and had all of us chuckling, including Connie. Laughter is good medicine every time. And so is companionship!

When a senior feels isolated from the outside world, loneliness and depression often follow. Staying in touch with family or friends is key to mental and physical wellness as you age. The problem many seniors face is that people they've been close to for years often move away, become sick or die. It can be difficult to continue staying socially engaged when so many drastic changes occur. A good resource available in almost all neighborhoods is the Senior Center which provides a variety of activities that appeal to many seniors and gives them a much needed sense of community.

Research has shown that older adults with strong social networks seem to have a higher quality of life, live longer and are healthier compared to those with little social support (Glass, Mendes de Leon, Marottolie & Berkman, 1999). Socialization has a positive impact on numerous areas, including blood pressure, memory and preventing depression.

A Vision Of Loveliness

Mary's situation was a sad and unusual situation because not only is she legally blind and confined to a wheelchair, but her son is also handicapped. It was the son who called us for help–he lives at home with his mother.

Mary was having great difficulty getting in and out of her bed or to the bathroom, and her son was no longer able to lift her because of his own disability. Often, he resorted to asking the neighbors for help getting his mother to bed at night. Needless to say, their daily lives were challenging—sometimes impossible.

The first thing we did was to recommend the use of a Hoyer lift (which is a device that assists people with limited mobility getting in and out of bed). A Hoyer requires little physical strength to operate. The next step was to bring in a caregiver, who arrives early to help Mary get out of bed, bathe and dress. She settles Mary in for the rest of the day, leaving a lunch plate nearby and some music playing on the radio. She leaves her with the phone within reach and makes sure there is nothing in the path of her wheelchair.

When Mary's son comes home from work later in the day, they have dinner together, and he is able to help her back to bed without difficulty thanks to the Hoyer lift (which was prescribed by her physician and covered by insurance). Both are extremely grateful that their stress has been greatly reduced.

Because Mary is unsteady on her feet, she has a fear of falling. According to the literature, those seniors who fall are two to three times more likely to fall again. Many older adults develop a fear of falling that causes them to restrict their activities. Coupled with Mary's visual handicap, she has great fear for her safety. Therefore, she is less apt to get out of her wheelchair. And of course, lack of mobility brings its own health risks, such as skin breakdown, incontinence, digestive slowdown, poor circulation, etc.

The list is long. But seniors like Mary can learn simple exercises that will help increase strength and balance. Eating well, relaxing and managing stress, and learning to cope with the stresses of everyday life help seniors to increase their productivity and their longevity.

There are seniors who are capable of leaving their homes for services, and those who are housebound; but there is help for seniors in both categories:

AARP: 1-888-OUR-ARRP: 1-888-687-2277
Academy of Nutrition & Dietetics: 1-800-877-1600
Eldercare Locator: 1-800-677-1116
National Council on Aging (NCOA): 1-571-527-3900
Alzheimer's Association 24/7 Help line 1-800-272-3900

Sometimes the hardest part of helping a senior is getting them to acknowledge they need the help and to take advantage of the people and facilities that are available to them.

We periodically hear from families that they are apprehensive approaching their parents about hiring a caregiver to come to the house. But we reassure them that when we meet our potential clients, we let them know that they will continue to be the boss in their own homes; that they are the ones still in charge. When seniors hear this, they often sigh with relief–since a fear all seniors understandably face is losing control of their lives. Our mission is to keep a senior in his or her home, for as long as possible, safely and with dignity. And most importantly, we treat your family like we would our own!

If you would like more information regarding our companion services, please call us at 718-720-7242 and mention this book. You can also email us at rnstaffingsolutions@gmail.com or visit our website www.rnstaffingsolutionsny.com.

It will be our pleasure to help you!

References:
National Alliance for Caregiving
AARP
National Institute on Aging
National Institutes of Health

HEALTHY EATING: THE GOOD, THE BAD AND THE UGLY

In America today we have a growing epidemic of Type II diabetes and obesity. They go hand in hand. The heavier a person becomes, the greater their insulin resistance, therefore the greater their risk of diabetes. Our seniors have been hit hard by this epidemic. According to the American Diabetes Association, between 1993 and 2001 there was a 36 percent increase in the diagnosis of diabetes in the population 67 years of age and older.

Diabetes means your blood glucose (often called blood sugar) is too high. It is well known that uncontrolled diabetes comes with a host of dreadful conditions. Diabetes is the one number cause of adult blindness; it can affect ones heart, kidneys, sexual function, ability of wounds to heal, which can result in amputations. Diabetes can also be fatal.

I've been a registered dietitian for over 20 years and a certified diabetes educator for over a decade. Since 1999, I've had a private practice specializing in diabetes. It's frustrating to me that there is so much misinformation about the nutritional management of diabetes given to our seniors. Every diabetic seems to have a friend or loved one offering bad advice about how to eat.

I can't count the number of times a diabetic senior has told me that he or she has been told that it's okay to have that large piece of cake because it's sugar free! (But it's loaded with carbohydrates that will break down into simple sugars–so it has to be treated as a source of sugar.) Patients have even told me that toasting bread takes out the carbohydrates. Or that breaking cookies into smaller pieces reduces their calories–even if you eat every last piece!

Often when seniors think they're going to a nutrition-ist a diet expert for help that's not always the case. Anyone can call themselves a nutritionist because unfortunately, there are no laws regulating the use of this term; one or two courses in nutrition and a health food store clerk might call themselves a nutritionist and give advice about diets, diabetes and other medical conditions without any real education or training. According to the American Dietetic Association, "Registered Dietitians" (RD) are the food and nutrition experts who can translate the sci-ence of nutrition into practical solutions for healthy liv-ing. An RD uses their nutrition expertise to help individ-uals make unique dietary adjustments to create positive lifestyle changes".

Our food preferences begin early in life. In fact there are only four basic kinds of tastes: sweet, salty, sour and bitter. We eat for many different reasons. The first and most important reason should be to maintain our health and to provide our bodies with energy and fuel: like gas is for a car. We also eat to celebrate, like at weddings. We go out to eat with friends, some eat when they are sad and others eat, when they are happy. There are many things that influence our food choices including cultural beliefs, food preference, social and economic status and convenience. Changing the way one eats is the most challenging thing to successfully do. To be told after 40 plus years of eating and cooking a certain way that you need to change your habitual routine is extremely difficult, yet is can be done when you set your mind to it and have an Expert Dietitian on your team, like myself.

Some of the least effective advice comes from the *"diet police" these are friends,* loved ones, family or even professionals who try to ban diabetic seniors from eating certain foods without considering how they've been eating for over six decades. I know a son who insisted that his 103-year-old mother stop eating her beloved cookie with her tea. Of course the son should have taken into account his mother's age; advice to a younger senior is going to be different than to a 103-year-old.

Imagine trying to tell an Italian woman who's been having spaghetti every Sunday for almost 70 years that she can no longer have pasta in her diet. She wasn't able to envision banning pasta completely from her life. People with some sound advice, can enjoy eating the foods they are accustomed to while managing their diabetes.

A seasoned dietitian works with each diabetic client individually to come up with a realistic effective nutritional plan tailored to that client's own food preferences, age and life style. Food is a major source of pleasure and depriving a person of that pleasure is counterproductive, as opposed to helping them stick to a healthy lifestyle. Also it's necessary to take into account a senior's ability to provide meals for themselves. (I can even teach seniors how to be healthy on frozen meals, if they're only able to nuke their way through dinner.)

To a certain degree all seniors are more at risk of developing Type II diabetes than younger people because their pancreas, which naturally produces less insulin or the insulin that is produced, is less affective. Let me explain, if you have a car long enough eventually parts are going to wear out. The same is true with the human body. When people age they tend to gain weight. Weight gain exacerbates the problem; especially weight gain in the stomach area. Visceral fat or fat in the stomach area reduces the effectiveness of the insulin secreted by the pancreas.

Insulin is necessary to remove sugar from our bloodstream and get it into the cells, which require it. Think of all your cells as closed vaults with insulin as the key that unlocks them, allowing the sugar to flow in. Fat blocks the insulin, keeping the sugar in the blood and not allowing the cells to receive the nourishment they need. The result? Your blood has sugar in it, and therefore it is thicker. The higher your blood sugar and or the longer your sugar stays high, the greater the risk of developing complications from diabetes.

Diabetes can affect every part of the body from head-to-toe. Think of it this way, when your sugar is high your blood is thickened with sugar ("considered dirty"). Your kidneys work harder trying to "clean" the blood; that's why diabetics often get kidney damage which can result in kidney failure. Thick blood means your heart has to pump harder and your blood doesn't circulate as well– that's why you get high blood pressure and a whole host of other problems commonly associated with diabetes.

It is crucial for seniors to be educated about their blood sugar levels, the difference between "fasting" levels and post prandial or after eating levels. The ideal healthy blood sugar level "fasting" has been lowered. Years ago we believed a "fasting" level of 140 mg/dl (milligrams per deciliter) was healthy; then the number was lowered to 110 mg/dl. Now we consider 100 mg/dl the healthy number. The reason the fasting numbers have been adjusted over the years is, as we learn new information about diabetes management we now know complications can be prevented. We also need to keep an eye on what is too low, as that can cause an immediate problem, including feeling dizzy and fainting. It is important to note seniors may have different target glucose, based on several factors including their age, other medical conditions, appetite, ability to exercise and their ability to identify when or if their blood sugar is too low.

My goal working with seniors is to find creative ways to help them maintain their target numbers and control their blood sugar through developing a palatable food plan in conjunction with their medications –which means timing when their meals are eaten and their medications are taken so they peak or work best.

The good news is insulin and other diabetes medications have become much better. Life has become easier for diabetics to manage their medical conditions and lead healthy and happy years free of complications. Years ago you had to time your meals carefully around your insulin injection. So you had to live your life around your diabetes. Now we teach people how to enjoy their lives while managing their diabetes.

I often like to visit seniors at home so that I can get an accurate picture of how they live, what and when they eat, and all the medications they take, including, any over-the-counter medications and nutritional supplements. We come up with a nutritional plan together which should reduce their weight, controls their blood sugar and also incorporates the best times to take their medication, as well as when to test their blood sugar so that they can get the maximum benefit from their diabetic medicine.

Sometimes my job is simply to provide helpful information to my patients and to make medication recommendations to their physicians. The important thing is to make sure that a diabetic person is fully informed about nutrition. I can't tell you the number of patients who've come to me saying that the doctor told them to lose weight and limit their fat intake. But they've no idea what that means.

The following serving sizes may contain too many carbo-hydrates for a senior diabetic. If you are not a diabetic here are some quick tips to assist with portion size: a cup (8 oz.) is equal to a female's fist or tennis ball. Where a large male's fist may be as much as 1 ½ cups, or even 2 cups. A tennis ball equals one cup cooked rice, or the proper size of a fruit, yogurt or milk. A baseball equals 12 ounces which is the serving size of cold cereal or a baked potato. One half cup is the correct portion size for vegetable, fruit cup or apple sauce and ice cream. A suggestion for lunch or dinner might be to eat three ounces of fish or poultry, which is approximately the size of a checkbook or a deck of cards. 1 or 2 servings of veg-etables and a starch food, noted above. Another useful measurement is the tip of the thumb, which is approxi-mately one teaspoon, or the equivalent of a serving of oil or salad dressing. When cooking spaghetti, a nickel in diameter is approximately 2 ounces dry, and will yield 1 cup cooked spaghetti.

Ann, is a 62-year-old woman who came to me very upset at her doctor's advice. Ann told me her doctor had rec-ommended she consume more calcium because of the results of her bone density test. When Ann returned to her doctor for her follow-up visit 30 days later, she had gained 22 pounds! I asked Ann what changes she'd made in her diet. She proudly stated that she'd increased her calcium intake by eating a 1/2 gallon of ice cream a day!

Ann told me the doctor hadn't provided any information on calcium rich foods, and she thought eating a 1/2 gallon of ice cream would be an enjoyable way of getting calcium. I explained to Ann that she could get calcium from eating greens such as collards, broccoli, spinach, turnips, also low-fat milk, and low-fat plain yogurt, cottage cheese, tofu, sardines with bones, anchovies, sea vegetables and beans. Ann was very grateful and excited to know that an intake of calcium didn't have to make her gain weight. She was also happy when she lost the weight, as quickly as she gained it.

Whether a senior walks into my office or I go on a home visit, I emphasize that I'm not judging; I'm teaching them and I can only do that if I know what they're eating. It is important to be respectful and give that person a voice in any plan that's devised to manage their medical condition, including diabetes. This actually increases compliance and results in better outcomes.

When I do a home visit, I ask the patient if they're comfortable letting me open the pantry and the refrigerator. I have found several problems that are common when I inspect a senior's kitchen–some related not just to diabetes but to overall health. Frequently seniors have in their pantries canned goods that are long past their expiration date and even bloated, indicating that it would be dangerous to consume them. It is difficult for seniors because cans are sometimes pushed to the back of shelves and the expiration dates are hard to see at a glance. I recommend rotating the cans and marking the expiration dates in large letters with black magic marker–the same with frozen foods.

Sometimes ironically as we get older, we eat more like teenagers: Macaroni and cheese from a box, pretzels, toast, cereal and the list goes on. I understand it; seniors who were once used to cooking for the family or sitting down to a family meal now often live by themselves. It's hard to adjust to cooking for one and lonely to eat alone. There's a nostalgic pleasure and ease in returning to junk food.

Sugary drinks such as soda, ice tea, and fruit punch are a big problem, and seniors are not surprised when I point this out. But they are surprised when I educate them on the dangers of juices, even those without sugar added. The media so often goes overboard in exaggerating the health benefits of a food such as juice. And seniors are caught unaware of its hidden dangers—especially for diabetics. It's amazing how much fruit needs to be crushed for an 8 oz glass of juice, ie. 8 to 9 apples for one glass of apple juice. For carrot juice, the amount is staggering–about 30-48 carrots for an 8 oz glass! Who can eat 30 carrots? And when you drink that glass of juice you're not getting the fruit or vegetables fiber which helps you absorb its sugars. It is a great surprise to all my senior patients when, I tell them that a diabetic's body doesn't know the difference between the high amounts of sugars you consume in juice or those in soda.

In addition grapefruit juice (as well as grapefruit) often interacts with various medications.

We are bombarded with food advertisements. It is important to note food manufactures have one mission. That mission is to sell their products regardless of their nutritional value. Studies have shown that more than half of television advertisements are related to food. In addition most of the commercials are for fast food, beer candy/chocolate, chips, milk and milk products such as cheese, yogurt, and sugary breakfast cereals. The majority of advertised foods on television are high in fat and sugar.

There are numerous commercials for nutritional supplemental drinks targeted at seniors. The nutritional supplements are not for any senior, especially a diabetic, who is battling their weight. These drinks are overloaded with calories. Unless you actually need to gain weight, and you are not eating food, drinking a nutritional supplement is only going to make that person gain unwanted weight. It's the equivalent of drinking a cup of whole milk and taking a vitamin pill. The misleading ads go on and on... A popular new fad is for a company to advertise that their soup, chips, etc., now contain sea salt instead of regular salt. Sea salt or regular salt–still should be limited, if you're a diabetic with high blood pressure.

I identify for seniors, which foods are healthy and good for them to eat, which they are better off staying away from or limiting. In addition to sugar, most simple starches such as bread, rice, potatoes, and noodles should be limited since they break down directly into sugar in the body. And of course trans-fats, saturated fats and high caloric foods keep weight on. A diet rich in fruits and vegetables, whole grains, low-fat calcium and lean proteins is ideal.

My patients are encouraged when they realize that starting with small changes often makes a real difference. One of my very first patients in the diabetes clinic was a feisty woman, Dee. It was obvious she did not want to see me and was annoyed at her doctor for referring her. Dee was "pre-diabetic." She was 4ft. 10in. and weighed 168 lbs. I explained that her excessive weight caused insulin resistance, which ultimately would result in diabetes and its complications.

When I asked Dee which dietary changes she was willing to make, she didn't respond. I offered her three choices: she could increase her water intake to at least 64 ounces a day, have two vegetables a day or limit her breakfast either to the one at home or the one at work. She chose the third option and returned in 4 weeks for a follow up appointment. Dee was ecstatic that she'd lost 18 pounds. I continued to work with her, she lost more weight, and she never developed diabetes.

As I have said, I try to work with folks individually so that they can still enjoy foods, a significant part of everyone's day. An interesting fact is, as we age the number of taste buds we have decreases. For many seniors, foods don't taste right, and they generally claim to need more salt seasoning. I tell people it is okay to use any seasonings but not salt. Fresh herbs, pepper, garlic and other seasonings are fine, but not garlic salt, as it is 50% salt. I also advise against salt substitutes, as often these are high in potassium, another possible concern for a diabetic person.

I would never say "never" to a food. Even fast food can be incorporated into a healthy diabetic's diet, if it's done occasionally, and the portion size is controlled. A McDonald's Happy Meal is the exact portion people should be eating as long as you don't get a regular soda with it. (You can even have the fries–without salt.) Healthy food options are available in fast food restaurants, such as chicken wraps and salads. Wendy's has a meal of a tremendous baked potato with a medium chili that a senior can divide into two or three meals.

Coming up with a strategy for a diabetic senior isn't just about talking to them; it's also about listening. I ask the senior to take me through their day—what time they wake up, what times they eat and what they like to eat during the day. As well as any activity they may do.

I have found ways to get a realistic picture of what people are eating. It is human nature to downplay, even fool ourselves about our bad habits–so I probe a little. I ask seniors when they last went grocery shopping, and would they mind if I see the receipt? If I find cookies and ice-cream had taken up a big chunk of the grocery bill, I've spotted a problem that I know I'll have to address.

A big part of my work with diabetics is familiarizing myself with a clients eating schedules to help them determine when the best times are for them to test their sugar, the best time to take medication, as well as how to make dietary changes when their sugar is too high.

Remember that sweet Italian lady who wanted to eat pasta on Sundays, as she'd done her whole life? She and I worked out a plan for her to do that safely. I told her to first test her sugar right before she had a bite to eat and then two hours after her first bite of food. After eating, her sugar shouldn't have risen more than 50 points.

But it went up 300 points! So I suggested dietary changes that she might make to reduce that number such as not eating the bread with her meal and adding more vegetables to slow the absorption of carbohydrates from the pasta. Now she safely and happily has her Sunday pasta.

It's also important for me to know which medicines my patients are taking to help them determine if the medications are working effectively and to help them properly integrate their diabetes medication into their daily life.

When I'm doing a home visit, I even want to look in medicine cabinets to see for myself, in case a patient has forgotten something. Or if a patient has brought their medicine to the office, I'll ask to see the actual bottle. I can't tell you how often medications are taken incorrectly. At times a medication might be prescribed as twice a day and the person only takes it once a day.

Not every diabetic takes insulin. Whether or not you use insulin or another type of medication depends on a variety of factors, including if you have other medical problems related to the diabetes, such as high cholesterol, high blood pressure, or kidney disease.

Many seniors are fearful of taking insulin; this most likely comes from the fact that years ago insulin was often prescribed too late--and it was therefore perceived as less effective. So it became associated with amputations and blindness. This isn't true. Insulin has its benefits in that it's easy to take, and it's natural to our bodies. After all our pancreas produces it and we can determine when the insulin will be working most effectively. Insulin is a diabetes medicine that bypasses the liver and kidneys, which is not true of other medications.

Insulin can't be taken orally, it must be injected. Many seniors are hesitant to inject themselves. Many of us have seen the commercial--a daughter at a big family dinner notices her elderly father's hand shaking--the same hand, we're told in voiceover, that he uses to inject himself with insulin. *What now?* The daughter is said to wonder, gravely concerned.

Well what now, is that in recent years, the medical profession has developed an insulin "pen," which is prefilled with insulin. It's easier to use for those with fine motor skill impairments and is associated less with pain at the injection site.

For those whose sugar is so out of control that they need multiple injections–maybe four or five a day– a better option might be an insulin pump. There is no surgery necessary for an insulin pump. It's no bigger than a pager and attaches to your body through a tube and is worn on your pants or in a pocket (like a cell phone). The insulin pump provides insulin throughout day. When you are about to eat you check your blood sugar and program the insulin pump to deliver insulin to cover what you are going to eat. I am a certified insulin pump trainer, and I've personally witnessed the pump's effectiveness, and the freedom it offers patients.

I encourage my patients to get a copy of their lab reports from their doctors. This helps me assess their sugar levels, and it is also a way for patients to take an active role in educating themselves about their own health. Seniors should have (lab results) blood tested for their fasting blood sugar levels and cholesterol yearly (including the total cholesterol, HDL or healthy/good cholesterol, LDL- bad or lousy a good way to remember l for lousy and triglyceride the ugly). If you have diabetes and high cholesterol, you have a greater chance of a heart attack. If your sugar and your triglycerides are high, you run a greater risk of pancreatitis.

I work with diabetic patients so they can control their diabetes, improve their overall health, and possibly lose enough weight to stop taking diabetic medication(s). I don't impose strict meal plans. Working closely with the diabetic community, I have learned that rigid meal plans are ineffective because when a patient feels too restricted they may want to cheat. Instead I like to leave patients with the skills they need to create healthy meals as they go.

I also discuss with my patients some of the biggest misconceptions about being a diabetic. Surprisingly, a popular one is that you can safely walk around barefoot or even in socks at home! Remember the higher your sugar the thicker your blood. Thicker blood can cause circulation problems, and can make the feet feel numb. People aren't even aware of this, and they believe they're safe in their own homes. Then they often step on something sharp like a staple or piece of glass, (from a glass or plate that broke months ago) and they don't even feel it. And in a worst case scenario, they now have a wound that won't heal and can lead to amputation.

In the end I tell my patients ironically that they are the lucky ones – because they know they have diabetes. While there are 27 million cases of diagnosed diabetes, it is estimated there are 54 million undiagnosed cases. Diabetes isn't a life sentence if you know about it. You can control it through diet and other smart lifestyle choices. But not knowing leaves you open to all the complications of uncontrolled blood sugar. Then it is literally a life sentence.

On another note, it is well known, nutrition is the cornerstone of many medical conditions including diabetes, hypertension, cardiac disease, kidney disease, various cancers, digestive disorders such as GERD, IBS, crohn's, celiac disease, diverticulitis / diverticular, gallbladder, malabsorption syndrome and anemia. In addition, nutrition is supportive therapy in inflammatory conditions, Alzheimer's and dementia as well as HIV/AIDS.

There are many diets we have all heard of such as the grapefruit diet, the cabbage soup diet and Mediterranean diet. Some have factual basis but may not be good for all conditions. For example, the Mediterranean diet can be a healthy way to eat with emphasis on plant based protein and heart healthy fats however this may not be beneficial for certain conditions. Other diets are often trendy and are not based in scientific evidence based findings and provide no actual benefit.

Before changing the way you eat it is always wise to discuss this with a credentialed professional who knows your medical condition and is familiar with your medication and how to interpret your laboratory results.

This is particularly important as in the case of multiple overlapping medical conditions. It is important to speak with an expert for proper direction. For additional information regarding getting healthier one meal at a time contact me at DebraSgross@gmail.com or call 917-670-1203

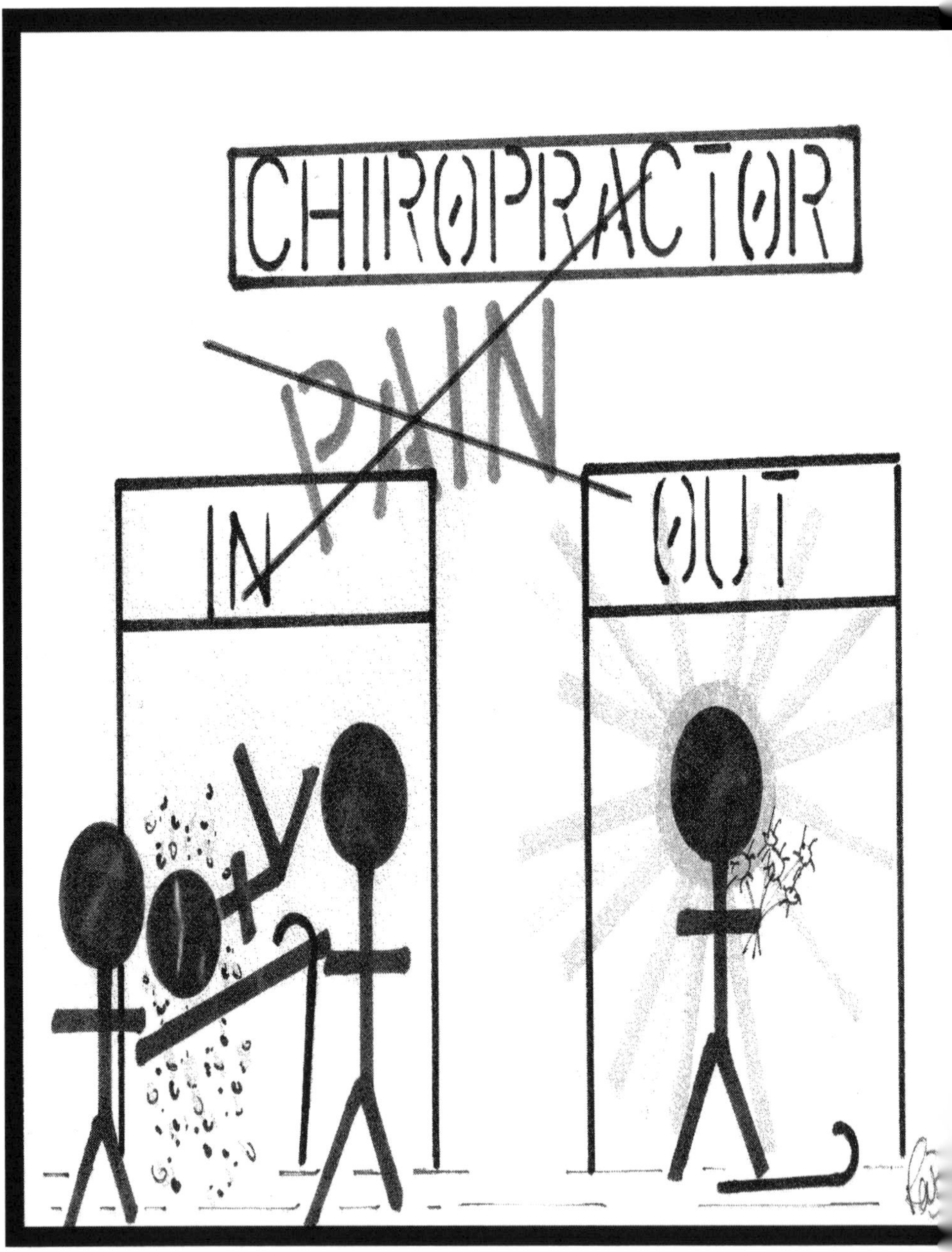
CHIROPRACTOR
PAIN
IN
OUT

NATURALLY HEALING FROM PAIN, AT ANY AGE

Mrs. Jones* looked every one of her eighty-eight years when she slowly and unsteadily walked into our chiropractic office, leaning on her cane for support. She came to us complaining of recent neck pain and stiffness. In addition, she had been receiving physical therapy for a lower back problem, but her walking wasn't improving. Her biggest concern though wasn't her walking. She wanted to drive safely.

I was surprised that a woman in her condition was talking about driving. Yet the more she spoke about herself, the more I realized that Mrs. Jones had been, until recently, a very independent lively woman. She had, however, also been suffering from pain for several years, which was getting worse and worse. What finally sent Mrs. Jones to a chiropractor was that she was about to make her yearly trip to Puerto Rico. She told me that she had always been a great driver, and in Puerto Rico, she really loved to drive to her favorite local hotspots.

In our office, Mrs. Jones couldn't even turn her neck–so driving was impossible. My examination revealed that Mrs. Jones had degenerative osteoarthritis in her neck. Also her back was hurting because she had lumbar spinal stenosis, which is a narrowing of the spinal canal.

Unfortunately osteoarthritis is very common in seniors. But as Mrs. Jones learned, seniors don't have to accept that they are helpless in the face of osteoarthritis or other degenerative spinal conditions common to seniors. And prescription medications–which only mask the underlying problem –are not the only way to relieve suffering.

Seniors can make these degenerative conditions much more manageable by staying active, practicing good nutrition and paying attention to posture and how they move-even while doing everyday ordinary activities such as getting in a car or vacuuming.

And it is very helpful for seniors to visit a chiropractor, who will make gentle adjustments to relieve pain and realign the body–as well as counsel seniors on healthy lifestyle choices. Chiropractic is a natural healthcare system that does not prescribe medication or perform surgery to fix spinal pain, instead we focus on correcting the structure of the spine to reduce pain and restore range of motion. We are trained to evaluate your muscles and joints to determine which ones aren't moving correctly and which muscles need to gain flexibility and strength. A spinal x-ray or MRI may be ordered to get a more detailed view of what's going on in your body so that we apply the appropriate treatment.

Chiropractic treatment techniques primarily involve manual therapies such as spinal adjustments, muscle therapies (such as massages, stretching, and trigger point release) and physiotherapy modalities (such as ice packs, electrical stimulation and ultrasound) to restore motion, reduce pain, and improve muscle function and joint mobility. Patients are given home exercises. Also, chiropractors are trained to rule out other pathologies and refer you to other health care providers if needed.

A recent literature review finds evidence that patients with neck pain enrolled in clinical trials reported significant improvement following chiropractic spinal manipulation, according to an August 2010 report in the *Manual Therapy Journal (1)*. Chiropractic manipulation improves joint flexibility thereby reducing muscle spasm and pain, and allowing you to get back to your daily activities so you can stay healthy.

Chiropractic treatments can be very effective for seniors, as was true in Mrs. Jones's case. The difference was remarkable, comparing the first time she visited our office and seeing her at her final therapy–when she was ready to drive around Puerto Rico!

The first thing a chiropractor does when any new patient comes into the office is diagnose, his or her problem. We sent Mrs. Jones to take a neck x-ray to rule out any diseases or other pathologies.

Then we gave her a physical exam including postural and biomechanical analysis of her spine. In layman's terms, this means we observed her posture–how she was standing and walking– for clues to her problems. Was she leaning forward? How were her joints? Which areas of her body didn't have motion? We then perform a physical examination and ask you to bend and move in different ways, we also test all your reflexes and see if you have good muscle strength throughout your body. It was clear from observing Mrs. Jones that she had problems with the joints in her lower back, pelvis and neck as well as very tight and weak muscles. We sent Mrs. Jones for a neck x-ray to determine how severe the arthritis in her spine was, and in her case, she had moderate osteoarthritis of her neck.

A trial period of treatment was designed for Mrs. Jones, as it is for all our patients. Given her age and the severity of her symptoms, we decided that it was realistic to evaluate her after six weeks. We hoped that within that time, Mrs. Jones would improve twenty five percent. But she exceeded our expectations!

The treatment plan was tailored to her age, her level of pain and the severity of her other symptoms. Spinal adjustments were made to Mrs. Jones's neck using an instrument, which restores alignment to the spine without twisting or turning it. (This technique is particularly useful on seniors because it's so gentle.) Mrs. Jones was also given muscle therapies such as massages and stretching. To treat Mrs. Jones's lower back, we used a technique called flexion-distraction, which was particularly helpful. The technique can be done very successfully on a frail patient. Mrs. Jones lay face down on a special table, and all she had to do was relax. The bottom half of this table gently lowered and stretched out her lower back. Mrs.

Jones said this technique felt great! And it's very safe to use. We also gave Mrs. Jones simple exercises to do at home and coached her on improving her posture.

Within a few weeks, Mrs. Jones was walking more quickly than before and only using her cane for support. She felt more energetic and was able to perform more errands without having to rest. We measured how far she could turn her head, and her range of motion improved with each treatment.

By the end of our treatment plan, Mrs. Jones had exceeded our expectations. She was walking more and needed her cane only when she was having an off day. She was also back to driving because she had enough mobility in her neck to check her mirror. When she left us, she was feeling and functioning well and was able to take her vacation. She could drive her car without worry or discomfort!

It may be surprising to some that chiropractors can deliver very safe effective treatments to frail seniors. Some think of "snap, crackle, pop" when they think of a chiropractor, or that they are going to have their backs "cracked." That's because of the audible sounds that certain adjustments make. But our profession is very sensitive to the needs of each patient who comes to us, and obviously an eighty-eight year old woman will be treated much more gingerly than a twenty-five year old.

Seniors commonly suffer from conditions that respond well to chiropractic treatments. Osteoarthritis is a common form of degenerative disease affecting the weight bearing joints such as the hips and spine. Lumbar spinal stenosis is a common cause of lower back pain in seniors.

We have 24 vertebrae in our spines, five in the lower back, twelve in the mid-back and seven in the neck. These bones are separated by intervertebral discs that are composed of a pulpy inside (nucleus pulposus) and tough outer fibers (annulus fibrosis) that interlock to hold the pulp inside. These discs are important for shock absorption and keeping the vertebra separated so the spinal nerves can exit freely at each bone and go to their respective destinations.

As we age, the discs lose height and start to deteriorate. We don't know exactly why–it might be natural wear and tear. Obesity, trauma to a joint and dislocation of a joint are some of the other factors that can contribute to this. Every senior is affected by this condition to some extent. The degree to which osteoarthritis is present varies from person to person.

When discs deteriorate, they are no longer nice and plump, but instead start bulging out into the spinal column. The result? They can press on the nerves exiting the spinal cord and cause sharp, radiating pain down your arms or legs. In cases such a spinal stenosis, weakness in the legs and arms may occur as well as losing the ability to turn and twist in different ways.

To visualize this process, think of a peanut butter and jelly sandwich. A disc is the peanut butter and jelly, and the bones are the bread. If you compress the bread, the peanut butter and jelly (the discs) will bulge out the sides of the bread (the bones), touching areas they shouldn't, i.e. the nerves.

Lumbar spinal stenosis is a progressive condition. People suffering from spinal stenosis might not be able to walk or stand for long periods of time, or bend to sit or stand. They can suffer leg weakness and cramps, stooping forward and/or pain.

However chiropractors can treat this condition by determining which areas of the spine may be lacking movement, then applying adjusting techniques to restore motion to affected joints. Muscles that are weak and tight also receive treatment. The condition improves, or at least, its progression slows. This is especially important for seniors, since if their condition doesn't deteriorate, they may avoid becoming wheelchair bound.

Mrs. Smith,* a seventy-five year old, walked into our office with her head hung low and lolling to the right side. And she limped. She couldn't walk properly because her right leg was so weak. She was experiencing such sharp, pinching pains in her upper back and shoulder that she could barely move her arm, and she couldn't sleep on her right side. She wasn't able to carry things. And the pain in her right leg was so severe she couldn't drive. She could only walk up stairs by lifting herself up with her left leg, because her right leg didn't have the strength to conquer the height of a step. And since she had also lost some of the nerve impulses that control the muscles of her right foot, she had to be careful walking upstairs because she would occasionally lose her balance.

To make matters much worse, Mrs. Smith's husband was dying. He was bedridden, and Mrs. Smith was his primary caretaker. She did everything for him, and she had probably been overdoing things for a long while. But like many patients her age, she did too much for too long. Then her problems hit her all at once.

She came to us desperate to try anything for some relief. Medications and physical therapy hadn't helped her at all.

A complete examination revealed something that might be startling to the layman–the acute pains she was suffering in so many different parts of her body came from two specific nerves. By evaluating the pattern of Mrs. Smith's pain, it was clear what was going on. These pinched nerves were causing a majority of her problems! You could trace them as they traveled, causing terrible pain in her right neck, arm and shoulder. Her right leg was so painful and weak because a pinched nerve had traveled all the way down her leg.

I explained to her that it might take a month or two to see real results because her condition, with its high level of pain, had been chronic (ongoing for at least a year) and it would take some time for her body to return to normal. I told her that she should expect only some mild decrease in pain in less than a month.

NATURALLY HEALING FROM PAIN, AT ANY AGE

When you experience an episode of pain, and it doesn't dissipate in a few days, seek a health care professional such as a chiropractor. Often patients make the mistake of ignoring an episode for weeks– or even much longer– and not seeking treatment. During this time you can be damaging your body further by doing your daily activities. And your pain may become chronic, which means it will probably take longer for you to heal.

We treated Mrs. Smith with chiropractic adjustments, muscle therapy and home exercises. (One very effective exercise done easily at home is to lie on your back and bring your knees to your chest, one knee at a time.)

Within two months, Mrs. Smith had made great strides. By the end of treatment, she was functioning one hundred percent! She could drive again, raise her right leg to walk stairs and carry packages. Most importantly, she didn't have pain! So of course her energy returned. And she had lost weight because walking was part of her prescribed treatment. (We suggest people take a proactive role in managing their condition.)

Mr. Allan, 63 year-old, came to our office plagued by chronic headaches and neck pain. At first glance, it was hard to believe that Mr. Allan suffered from any muscle weakness or tightness or that he was in need of any chiropractic treatment–since he'd been a Longshoreman for over twenty years and was still working part-time!

He was complaining, however, that he had headaches so severe that he was having trouble working at all. He was given a full spinal checkup–his posture was evaluated, x-rays were taken, his spine was palpated. It was determined he had multiple dysfunctional joints in his neck and upper back, and tight muscles that caused him to feel pain all around his shoulders.

After four weeks of adjustments on his back and neck, ultra sound, neck stretches, home exercises to strengthen his upper back and shoulders and counseling on posture, Mr. Allan had complete relief of neck pain and headaches. Now every month, he comes for a follow-up visit to maintain motion in his spine and neck–plus he says the treatments relax and energize him.

It is not surprising that Mr. Allan responded so well to chiropractic treatment. Despite the fact that he has always been very fit in certain respects, it's also true that Mr. Allan spent a lifetime using his body the way many seniors have–overusing strong muscles to compensate for weaker ones.

The cause of Mr. Allan's headaches was a common one. He was not used to holding his head in right alignment. Instead he jutted it forward. The head weighs between eight and eleven pounds, and if it's not correctly centered over the shoulders, its weight strains the muscles in the neck. The muscles become weak and short in the front and overstretched in the back. This signals pain receptors in the neck to fire. And a headache can be the result.

Chiropractors are dedicated to teaching our senior patients–and of course all our patients-how to maintain a healthy lifestyle. We counsel our patients on the importance of ergonomics–how to use one's body correctly. For example, we advise them not to sit on a soft couch that has no support; to vacuum in a lunge-like position (one leg in front of the other); not to twist their body when getting in or out of a car (but to swing their legs in or out).

We emphasize that exercise is imperative for everyone in order to maintain healthy cardiovascular and respiratory systems, as well as good muscle tone and flexibility in the spine and limbs. And exercise is great for reducing stress because it releases feel-good endorphins produced by your body for a "natural high." It is also an important way to ward off conditions such as osteoporosis. Your goal should be to walk three to four times per week, always starting on a flat surface. Wear comfortable supportive sneakers. Even if you can't walk far, it's important to go as far as you can. Even if you can't walk, rock in a rocking chair–it's therapeutic!

Every time you move, a joint becomes lubricated and stays more flexible. And every time you do weight bearing exercises, your bones build and remodel. Rocking chairs can benefit your legs and feet because you use your body to move back and forth and thus keep your joints mobile.

It is also vital to have a healthy and varied diet. Try to eat seasonal fruits and vegetables. Also buy organic produce and meats. Food raised organically does not contain harmful pesticides, chemicals and hormones. In addition, incorporate some form of protein at each meal to build and maintain muscle strength. Good sources of protein are lean organic meats, tofu, quinoa, eggs, etc. The most important ingredients to avoid in your diet are high fructose corn syrup, hydrogenated oils, artificial sweeteners and processed foods. These foods contribute to inflammation in your body because of the chemical reactions they produce. A good way to ensure you are choosing the right foods is to simply stay on the perimeter of the grocery store when you food shop. This is where all the fresh food is displayed such as in the produce isle, and the dairy and meat cases.

The best method for treating muscular and skeletal disorders is truly prevention. And if you do experience pain, you may find relief through chiropractic care. We see our dentists for checkups twice a year, our medical doctors at least once or twice a year. Spinal health is just as important. Your chiropractor will check your spine and let you know how it is functioning. We can determine if you need some postural or ergonomic advice, as well as how strong your muscles are.

Chiropractic care is extremely safe and effective for everyone –including seniors.

If you would like to receive more information on chiropractic care and what it can do for you, please feel free to call (718) 680-2222 and speak with our receptionist to schedule a complimentary initial consultation.

Reference
Manual Therapy, Volume 15, Issue 4 August 2010 pages 334-354
Manual therapy and exercise for neck pain: A systematic review

Jordan Millera, Anita Grossa, b, Jonathan D'Sylvaa, Stephen J. Burniec, Charles H. Goldsmith, Nadine Grahama, Ted Hainesb, Gert Brønfortd, Jan L. Hovinge

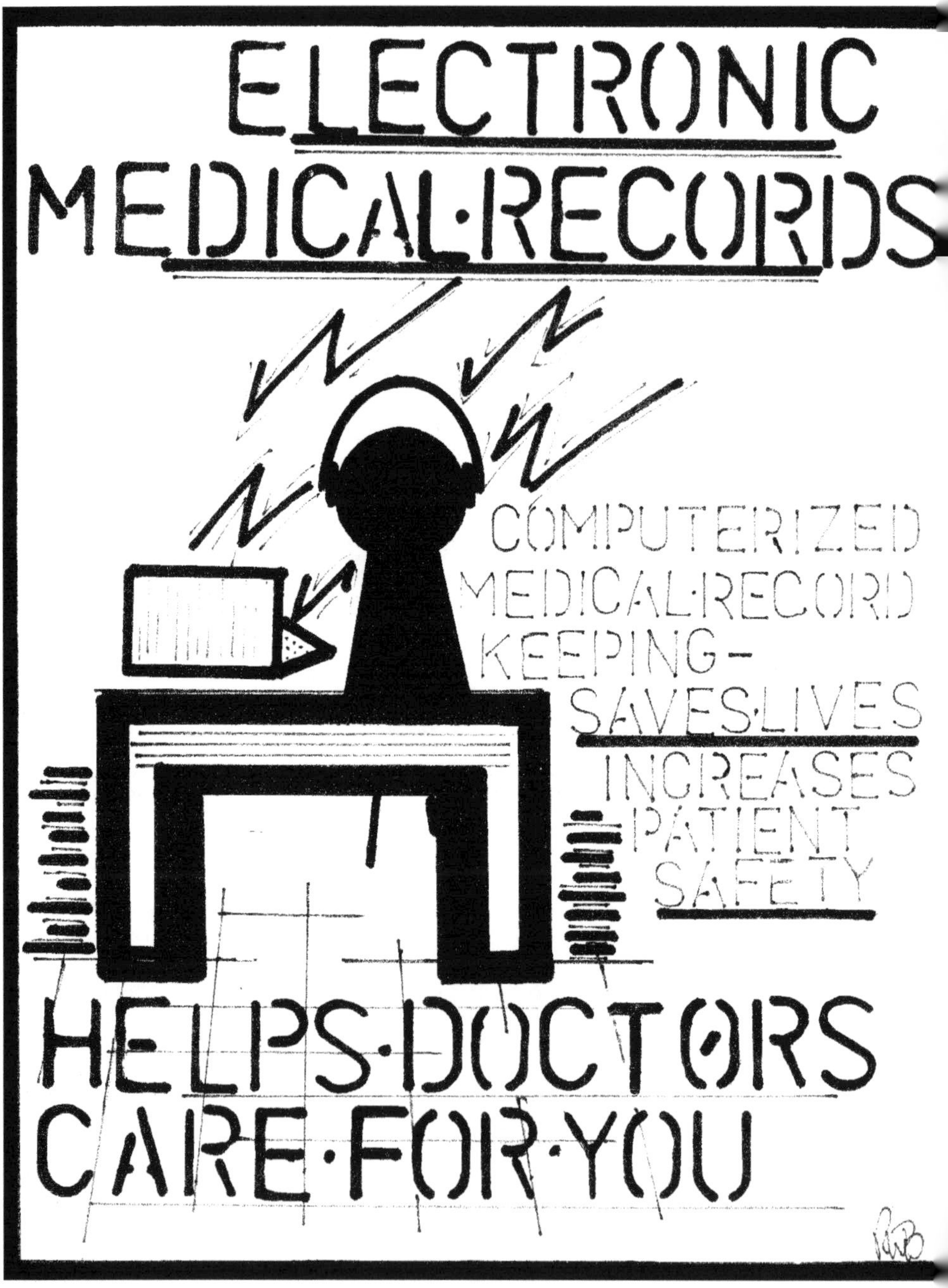
ELECTRONIC
MEDICAL·RECORDS
COMPUTERIZED
MEDICAL·RECORD
KEEPING–
SAVES·LIVES
INCREASES
PATIENT
SAFETY
HELPS·DOCTORS
CARE·FOR·YOU

ELECTRONIC MEDICAL RECORDS: WHAT WILL THEY MEAN TO US?

Imagine you become sick while vacationing in Paris and rush to a recommended doctor – who happens not to speak a word of English. (And you don't speak French.) But you give the nurse your name and a "patient ID number." And Voilà! On the Paris doctor's office computer, up pops your entire medical history–the name of your doctors in the United States, the list of medications you're taking, the results of your medical tests, x-rays, etc. And, not only that–everything has been translated into French!

Science fiction today, but in the not-too-distant future this scenario is likely to be science fact, as the internet and computers –with government incentives–are revolutionizing the way medical records are kept and creating new ways to access medical information.

In the near future our doctors and medical providers such as pharmacies and technicians will have our complete medical information at their fingertips. This means for example our pharmacists will glance at a computer screen and see all our medications. When we go for an x-ray or blood work, a technician can check a computer screen to make sure we're not being subjected to duplicate medical testing. In larger terms, statistical information compiled by computer programs will help develop "best practices" for our nation's doctors and hospitals to use in treating life threatening diseases and conditions such as aortic aneurysms, heart disease, and pneumonia.

This is certainly different from the way doctors' offices keep our medical records today. Many offices still enter your medical information on paper charts. Even if your doctor's office has computerized medical records, this is only the beginning of the revolution! Eventually computer medical records will become standardized and even all centrally located on a web server—which is how our French doctor will be able to see all your medical information. (Yes, the whole world is instituting standardized computer medical records; Ireland has 2,000 physicians doing this already. This is a worldwide Internet revolution in medical record keeping!)

How will this affect our lives? First let's look at the way things are today. Start at the beginning with a trip to a new doctor. The first thing that happens to all of us now is that we're told what to bring with us to the appointment of a doctor we've never seen before. Usually this includes our insurance card, photo ID and any other pertinent documents (such as other medical records). Special instructions might be given to us—

i.e. some offices tell us not to eat anything past midnight so the doctor can draw fasting blood.

We arrive at the office and usually find it filled with patients already waiting. As a new patient, we're handed a stack of forms to complete. These forms ask for a lot of information including: Name, address, past medical history, allergies, emergency contact, date of birth, social security number, employer, medications we take, surgical procedures we've undergone and their dates, and the reason for the visit. We hand over our insurance card so that a copy can be made. We sign all kinds of authorizations allowing the release of information to the insurance company so that the doctor will be paid. We acknowledge that if the insurance company doesn't pay, we will be responsible for the bill.

As we wait our turn, we watch a beehive of activity in the waiting room. Appointments are being scheduled, patients are called in by lab technicians, co-pays are collected, bills are copied to submit to insurance companies, new appointments or referrals are given by the front desk.

When our turn finally comes, a nurse usually takes our blood pressure, pulse, temperature and weight and writes it down on a chart. Since it's our first time at the office, the nurse doesn't know if these stats have fluctuated over time. (Unless we're savvy enough to remember bringing or faxing ahead our medical records from our other doctors.)

When we see our new doctor, he or she asks us why we're there, examines us, draws blood, orders an EKG or PFT- maybe an X-ray. (We might have had these tests recently, but again without any records in front of him or her, the doctor won't know what these test results were.) He or she listens to our heart and lungs and looks in our eyes and ears. The doctor reviews the list of medications we wrote down on one of the forms. (And we hope we remembered them all–or were so organized, we actually brought a list with us!) Our past medical history is reviewed as well as our family's medical history.

During the exam, the doctor may be writing notes by hand or talking into a tape recorder, which will later be transcribed. (Maybe this doctor is imputing his or her notes directly onto a computerized medical chart but the majority of doctors still have paper charts.) After the exam, the doctor might tell us to call in a few days for lab results or to make an appointment for a follow-up visit, or we might be handed a few prescriptions written in the doctor's barely legible scrawl. (Or if we're lucky, the prescription is a computer printout.) Often, we're handed a 'super-bill' that will be sent to the insurance company, and we're directed to give it to the desk on our way out.

When we go to the exit desk, the receptionist digs through a pile of charts to find ours and make sure that we've taken care of everything... picked up referrals, paid co-pays, requested any forms we need such as a return- to-work note etc.

But as we go back into the waiting room, we notice someone still sitting there who had arrived before us. We soon find out that their chart is misplaced. (No, this office does not yet have computerized charts.) So the front desk is creating a new 'temporary' chart. We realize that if the patient is going to this doctor for a follow-up visit, the doctor will not have the patient's previous notes, test and/or lab results available for the patient's visit today.

Now we drive to our favorite pharmacy and fill the prescriptions. The pharmacists look at these prescriptions and talk amongst themselves: "Can you read what the doctor wrote? What does this say?" They might have to call the physician's office to find out what drug we are supposed to be given. If we've filled prescriptions in different pharmacies, there's no way to check which other medications we take for any possible drug interactions.

A few weeks later, we visit a new referral doctor. When we walk up to the front desk and announce ourselves, we're handed a stack of forms...Name, address, emergency contact, allergies, social security, etc. Sound familiar?

The Future is Now and Just Around the Corner
The government has mandated that most physicians and hospitals have electronic health records and/or electronic medical records (EHR/EMR) in place by the year 2015. This doesn't simply mean that doctors' records must be computerized, but also that the information is entered into standardized templates. At present 40 percent of doctors use these "certified" standard computer templates nationwide.

Though this is still a minority of doctors in the country, the increase in usage is extraordinary when you consider that in 2010 only 19 percent of doctors' offices were using them. The government has been providing doctors with incentives to put these "certified" electronic records in place.

Our medical history and vital signs will be entered into these computerized medical charts. Physician notes will be checked off using a template or dictated into a program that will enter the data into our charts. Lab requests and prescriptions will be sent electronically. When you go to your pharmacy, they will have already received your prescription by email or fax. It will be in a printed format that is entirely legible. Some pharmacies today, such as Rite Aid and Walgreens, are already beginning to institute this system. Your lab results will be sent back electronically and attached to your electronic chart.

Bills will be sent directly to insurance companies, which is wonderful news to those of us who still struggle with filling out our own paper claims.

Though the government is not requiring all the components of the nationwide standardized medical record keeping system to be in place by 2015, the goal is that soon thereafter, all our healthcare information will be stored on a secure, encrypted web based site, much like the ones that banks use.

This will have a myriad of uses. When you arrive at that specialist's office in the not-too-distant future, they'll be able to see all your information and any medical evaluations and tests that were done previously by looking up your medical records online. Even if you're traveling to a foreign country, and you go to a hospital, they'll be able to log onto the system and see all your healthcare data–and it will be interpreted into the language of the country that you're visiting!

Pharmacies will know every medicine you take because all medications will be listed under your name regardless of the pharmacy that you filled them at. Possible drug interactions or incompatibility will be identified and prevented. Allergies will be clearly indicated.

The ultimate goal: Your entire health record complete and in one place so that all physicians will treat you based on the same information. And you too will have complete knowledge of your own medical history at your fingertips; so that you can look at it in much the same way you check your banking statements online today.

The Center for Medicare and Medicaid Services has been behind the big push for these standardized EHR/ EMR (electronic health records) because they will also serve another vital purpose. The CMS will have the ability to mine these records for data that will help them develop "best practices," for a whole host of medical conditions and diseases.

Imagine this–standardized electronic data sent directly to the CMS from thousands and thousands of hospitals on how they treat patients who come into their emergency rooms complaining of chest pains. The CMS analyzes this data to determine which treatments result in the lowest mortality rates–such as giving patients an

aspirin immediately and then sending them for an electrocardiogram. (The CMS has been pushing to develop
"best practices" in a variety of areas since the '80s but
systemized computer information is expected to expedi-
ently speed up and fine-tune this task.)

The goal is for the CMS to come up with standards
of care that will be instituted throughout the country–so
that no matter where you live, or which hospital or doctor
you see, you will always be given the most effective proven
medical treatments. The savings will be tremendous not
just in terms of dollars but more importantly in lives saved.

The CMS is concentrating on developing standardized
care for certain illnesses and conditions with high mortality rates such as influenza, heart failure, aortic aneurisms,
diabetes and pneumonia, and developing standardized
quality care to reduce fatalities caused by common medical mistakes made in hospitals and nursing homes.

Privacy and Security

The main concerns about creating internet-based medical
records are privacy and security. There are ways to deal with
these issues. Access can be given only on a need-to-know basis. The receptionist at the doctor's office will have a different access level from the nurse practitioner, who will have a
different access level from the pharmacist, and so on.

All information will of course be encrypted. Much
of our personal information is already online–from
our bank records to our credit card bills. And so much

sensitive or even top-secret governmental information has already been computerized–clearly this is the wave of the future. In addition, electronic health records will be backed up and safely stored off site so they can be recovered in case of a disaster.

Pros and Cons

Though there is currently an ongoing debate regarding the use of EHR/EMR, the pluses and minuses are readily identifiable. According to George W. Bush in his 2004 State of the Union Address, "By computerizing health records, we can avoid dangerous medical mistakes, reduce costs and improve care."

The positive reasons to have an electronic health record are many:

- Our designated healthcare providers will be able to access and share information regarding our medical conditions.
- Our files will be complete and organized.
- The potential for drug interactions will be minimized because all our medications will be listed in one place and will be current.
- Unnecessary testing will be greatly reduced.
- A comprehensive diagnosis will be available because our medical history, family history, past surgeries, allergies, etc. will all be brought onscreen by tapping a keyboard.

- Ultimately, we will be able to have modified access from our own computers to our records so that we can insure their accuracy.
- We will no longer need copies of our charts or results when we see another doctor or seek a second opinion.
- The electronic health record will be mineable to develop "best practices" for treating serious illnesses and conditions in the general population.
- ALSO, the electronic health record will be mineable to isolate any aspect of our record for our own individual purposes. This includes diagnoses or test results. An emergency room physician will be able to compare our present electrocardiogram with the one performed in our doctor's office several months prior. The same will be true for chest X-rays, lab results, etc.
- Lab results can be displayed on a summary graph indicating how well such things as our cholesterol or blood sugar are being controlled over a given time period.

The potential negatives of electronic medical records include:

- If a mistaken or inaccurate entry is made in our file, it can no longer simply be erased or deleted.

A correction or an edit will have to be entered acknowledging the error.

- We are concerned our health records will fall into the wrong hands. We don't want hackers or unauthorized people getting access to our personal health and identity information.

- We don't want the government or other entities such as insurance companies to use our medical records intrusively.

Conclusion

In the end, the positive reasons for having an electronic health record clearly outweigh the negative ones. Safety and improved healthcare are the ultimate goals. By decreasing the number of extra tests performed, we reduce the risks and costs that result for unnecessary testing. How often have we heard stories about a friend or loved one who went for a 'routine test' and ended up in the hospital or worse as a result of a medical error or drug reaction?

The number of injuries or deaths per year related to medical errors are staggering. For example, a 2006 follow-up to a 1999 Institute of Medicine study found that medication errors are among the most common medical mistakes, harming at least 1.5 million people every year.

According to the study, 400,000 preventable drug-related injuries occur each year in hospitals, 800,000 in long-term care settings, and roughly 530,000 among

Medicare recipients in outpatient clinics. The report stated that these are likely to be conservative estimates.

In 2000 alone, the extra medical costs incurred by preventable drug related injuries approximated $887 million – and the study looked only at injuries sustained by Medicare recipients, a subset of clinic visitors. None of these figures take into account lost wages and productivity or other costs. One can only imagine what current statistics would show as we, the baby boomer generation age and begin to have an impact on our healthcare system.

Quality and Safety! These are the operative words for our healthcare system in the future. Standardized computer medical records will bring us closer than ever in our nation's history toward achieving these goals.

Our company, MaxiReturn Services, helps physicians' offices choose the EMH/EMR system that's right for them. We also train staff to use the system, stressing the importance of privacy and adherence to all HIPAA (Federal privacy) regulations. And we help hospitals in their conversion to an electronic format, with a focus on training and supporting their staff.

If you know a hospital or physician's group in need of help with an EMR/EHR system, please tell them about us. We can help your doctor make the required transition from his paper charts to the 2015 requirements and beyond as painlessly and as efficiently as possible. We work with everyone on this push into the electronic medical record-keeping frontier– from single practitioners to large hospitals. And right now is the time to do so because there are government incentives to subsidize costs.

So, if you know a physician or a hospital in need of an electronic health record, please have them contact me, Mary Maroney, at 718-720-7244 or 917-364-3449.

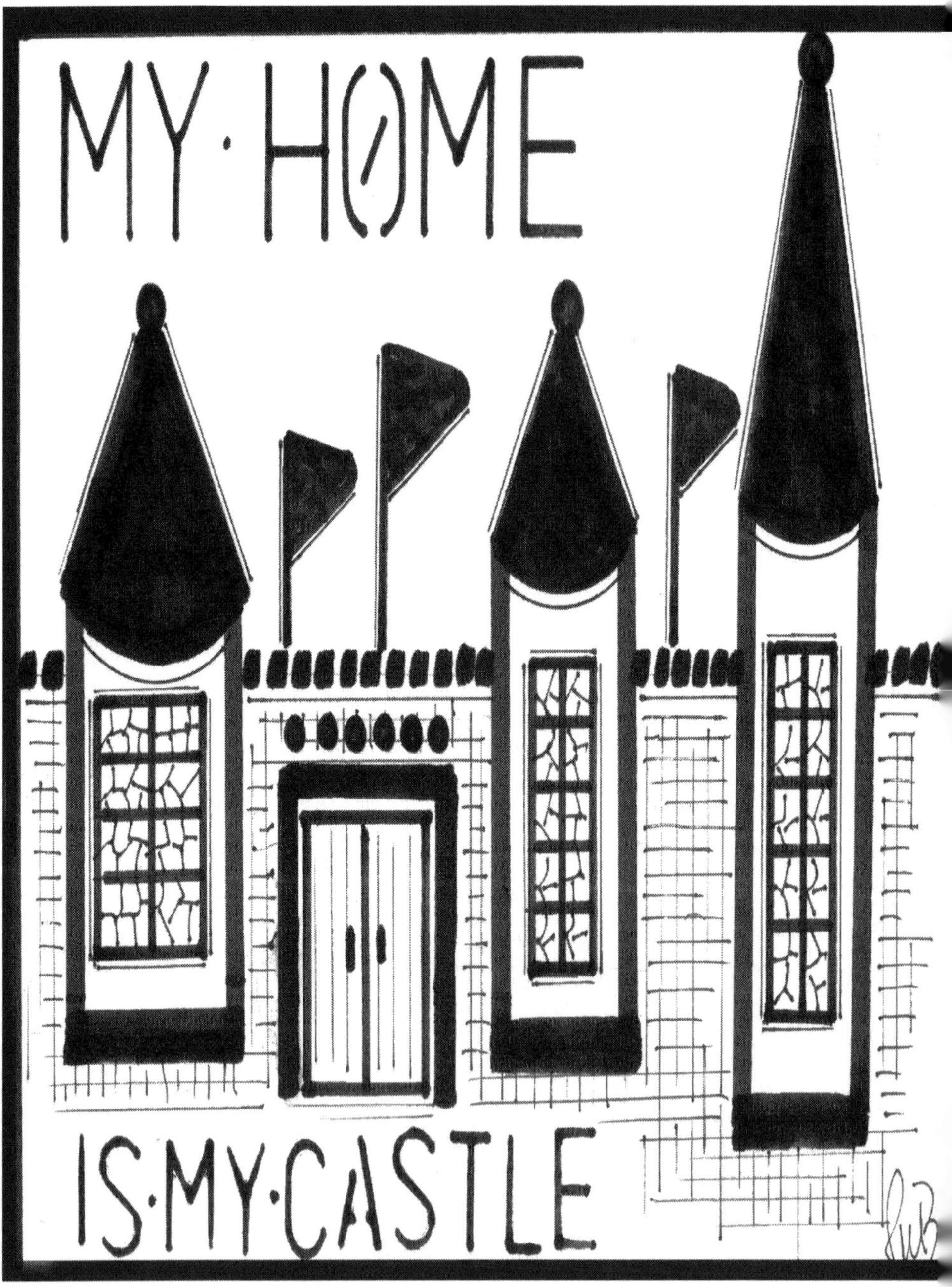
MY·HØME
IS·MY·CASTLE

MY HOME IS MY CASTLE

I remember learning in college we have several basic needs one of which is shelter. Shelter is a basic need and a basic need which when acquired in the right way can create great wealth. Many folks dream of home owner-ship and for many it remains only a dream. Proper finan-cial planning should cover the importance of planning for home ownership. Many of our parents and grand-parents purchased a home in their 20's or even 30's. By doing so they have been able to realize gains in equity, in many cases of hundreds of thousands of dollars, espe-cially if they reside on the East Coast in the NYC or the Long Island area.

The ownership of real estate has been one of the greatest creators of wealth in this country and home ownership is usually the largest single asset most folks have. That is why it is so important that, that asset be protected as discussed by attorney Robert Howe in his earlier chapter. This house can be used as a springboard to jump-start the financial success of future generations in a family. This may be one of the reasons why so many have heard the term money goes to money. In many cases, a substantial down payment is needed to purchase a home, along with the necessary income to qualify for a mortgage if a mortgage is needed.

SENIORS GET YOUR DUCKS IN A ROW

One of the few people lenders will approve of, who can give a gift of a down payment in the purchase of a home are parents and grandparents. Other folks are looked upon by lenders as giving a loan that needs to be repaid.

In selling houses one of the things I try to make my clients very aware of is the amount that is offered, is not the only factor that must be examined. This reminds me of a recent situation with a client I'll call John. John was only in his 70's and had not taken the time to make sure his affairs were in order. He had been having some health issues and decided to put his house on the market. Because of the health issues John wanted to sell quickly so he could enjoy the equity, he had built up over the years. With that said, I needed John to understand, to close quickly we would not only need a purchaser with the right financial status, we might also need to price the house slightly below the retail market at the time. The home was in a very up and coming neighborhood and as soon as the home was put on the market, we had many offers. My job is to not only present the offers to John, it is also to look at the financial picture painted by the person making the offer and discuss that with John. Since I have both a real estate salesperson's license and a license to originate mortgages, I tend to have a better understanding of which offers might present a better or smoother closing process for John. This does not mean a client will listen. John had purchased his home for 74,000 in 1978 and in just the last ten years, his home's value had more than doubled. His house worth about $350,000 back in 2005 was now worth over $600,000 in 2014. That was not enough for John, so he turned down a very nice cash offer that could have closed in 14 – 30 days. John accepted an offer that would get him an additional $35,000 on the sale. However, this purchaser unlike the cash investor insisted he wanted the house delivered vacant and there were tenants living in the home that were not ready to move. John needed to evict the tenants and this as some of you may realize became a lengthy process. Not only did John want to enjoy the money he had coming to him he also wanted to put money in an account that would have his sister's name on it so should anything happen she could easily have access to it. If he were to pass, she could have the funds right away.

Well, in the midst of all the processes of getting a contract signed and the purchaser applying for a loan through a very reputable lender, John's health took a turn for the worst. He never put together a power of attorney giving his sister the ability to complete the transaction and nor did he have a will. The entire deal fell apart and John was never able to enjoy the equity that had built up in the home throughout the years.

Danny another client was referred to me by an attorney. His mom owned her home free and clear. She had wanted to get a loan on the property, which was held in a trust. Because of the way the trust was worded none of the lenders they had spoken with were willing to make a loan against the property. Even though the home was in a trust, we were still able to sell the home. After the sale of the home, the proceeds were put in the trust; through the trust the trustee then purchased a home of lesser value for her. This now allowed for excess funds that gave her the ability to enjoy her re-maining years.

Sometimes selling the home and renting is the right thing to do. Lucille was a client of mine that this worked out well for. She had purchased her home about 20 years prior, and although she had done a reverse mort-gage five years ago to do some renovations she still had a nice chunk of equity left. Although Lucille had a cou-ple of hundred thousand dollars left when all was said and done, she did not have enough to enjoy the life-style she wanted. One of her daughters had moved to Florida several years ago and that was making Lucille think about moving to that area. Lucille did not like to fly so visiting her daughter was a bit of a chore since every time she decided to visit the area she would hop on a train. She was able to find a place in a brand new development. The new apartment had 2 bedrooms and 2 baths with a little lanai. She just loved her apartment however she did have to make some adjustments. Living in Brooklyn all these years she had taken for granted the close proximity to everything and ease of a great mass transit system. After the move, Lucille called me one day because her complex had asked for her up-dated info so they could renew her lease for the follow-ing year. She needed her social security award letter. So, she called me to find out what to do. Many of my clients have been with me for years and continue to keep in touch with me even after a mortgage transac-tion or real estate sale has been completed. In Lucille's case, we were having a real good laugh as we discussed what her journey to the Social Security office in Florida would entail. She was refusing to spring for cab fare for the thirty-mile journey to the Social Security office. She went on to tell me about her friend who had to take 3 buses to get there. She was insisting that she would just as soon take a train back to Brooklyn to go to the social security office here because she knew exactly where it was. I could not stop chuckling as the tears of laughter rolled down my face and she kept telling me I was crazy if I thought she was going to go 30 miles to the Florida office. In the end I had convinced Lucille to either get her daughter to go with her, however that would mean taking another day off of work or she could take a cab or perhaps take a new friend to lunch after they drive her to the SS office. She opted to get a friend to drive her there. Afterwards they went for lunch and that has created a great bond with a new friend and increased her fellowship with a local church in the area. From time to time, we still laugh about this. She loves the warm weather and although it is not as easy for her to get around since she does not drive, she has decided the move for her was the best thing she could have done. The moral of this story is if you are going to move to a completely new area don't forget to take care of your social security mailing address before you go, even if you have direct deposit.

Some of the clients I have worked with have only dealt with me in the capacity of selling their home. That is also all they were interested in having me get involved with at the time. Even though I had mentioned to one couple Joan and Bob that they should contact their medical insurance provider before they just move and later figure it all out. I had heard from them months after the move. They had called me because they had tried to make some doctors appointments for their annual check up. After calling their insurance provider, they were told they need a new plan for the area they are now living in. On top of that they were told that the union plan they had was not available where they were now living and once they opt out of the plan they can not get back in. You need to know what you will need to know before the time comes to make a decision to change things. In the case of Joan and Bob they still had coverage in case they had to go to the emergency room however this was really stressing them out when they were supposed to be having the time of their lives.

If you are selling a multi family property, you should really check with a tax advisor before selling. Many times, there are taxes that will be due and you should have an idea as to the numbers prior to selling. Your accountant might have been depreciating the building and therefore the tax basis might be different from what you might think it is. In addition, you might be eligible to do what is referred to as a 1031 exchange on a commercial property however this involves some prior planning in identifying another property within certain time constraints as well as closing on the new property within a certain period. This is something that should definitely be discussed with an accountant who understands how a 1031 exchange works.

Some folks think, why should I hire a real estate professional to sell my home when I can do it on my own? I can understand why they might think this way. Everyone wants to save where they can or get a buy. 88% of sellers were assisted by a real estate agent when selling their home, according to the 2013 National Association of REALTORS® Profile of Home Buyers and Sellers. The reason for this is there is a lot more involved than normally meets the eye.

What do you think a person is thinking when they contact someone with a, for sale by owner property? I'll tell you that their first thought is oh good I'll save the real estate commission since there is no realtor involved. On top of that, because you are so closely involved in the transaction it may be difficult for you to be rather matter or fact with these buyers. As a professional in the industry with a lot of experience negotiating with folks, negotiating is second nature to me. That makes a huge difference when you want the right price for your property. There are also many legal ramifications a person selling there home may encounter, such as what rules apply when it comes to discrimination and there are many that apply that I'm sure you do not realize apply. In addition, when I list a property I have connections not only with my sphere of influence, I also have a network of thousands of other Realtors® through our affiliation with Multiple Listing Services.

We are professionals adding a layer of security and peace of mind for you. We handle setting up the scheduling with you so that you are not in a position where you are fielding the large volume of calls we usually need to tend to. We work with your schedule and set appointments accordingly.

Recently one of my sellers insisted their home was in great shape and did not think they needed a home inspection done prior to selling. Well let me tell you if someone is buying a home for hundreds of thousands of dollars or even several million for that matter they will want to do a home inspection. A home inspection is relatively inexpensive in comparison to what I've seen people give away to get their deal closed because the buyer has come back and said you need to reduce the price by thousands of dollars or I'm not closing because you have some type of defect with your property. If this comes up at a point where a seller has already made their plans to move somewhere else and/or does not have the funds available at the time of the issue to make the repair it can be more costly to give a price reduction. In addition, at this point in the transaction there might be time constraints on both sides. Sometimes you might think putting in a new kitchen to get the right price is a great idea, then you find out the main beam to the house is in jeopardy and the buyer wants a ten grand reduction. It will only cost you a couple thousand to fix. Because you had spent the excess funds on the kitchen, you no longer have the funds available. So, what do most sellers do then? You got it; they reduce the price by 5x times what it might have cost to fix the problem in the first place. If only they had hired a home inspector for a few hundred dollars, they could have gained thousands.

If you know of anyone who is looking to sell their home and would like a *Free* consultation and market analysis prior to guessing at what they should do, please have them contact me. Annette Fisher, CSA, SRES, Real Estate Salesperson BRESRE Realty Inc. Cell: 347-291-7479. CSA, Certified Senior Advisor, SRES®, Seniors Real Estate Specialists. Also, I was the 2016 President for the Women's Council of Realtors Brooklyn.

MY NAME:

EMERGENCY CONTACT: _____ PHONE: _____

PRIMARY DR.: _____ PHONE: _____

PHARMACY PHONE: _____

BLOOD TYPE: _____ RELIGION: _____

Allergies & Medical Problems:

Date	Weight	Glucose	LDL Choles.	HDL Choles.	Triglyc.	Blood Pressure

Medications	Dosage	Times per day

Recent Hospital Admissions

Date	Hospital

Living Wishes

I, _____

Hereby appoint: _____

Address: _____

Phone: _____

as my health care agent to make all health care decisions for me and direct my attending physician to withhold or withdraw treatment that serves only to prolong the process of my dying. If I should be in a incurable or irreversible mental or physical condition with no reasonable expectation of recovery.

_____ **I do not want cardiac resuscitation.**
INITIALS

_____ **I do not want mechanical respiration.**
INITIALS

_____ **I do not want tube feeding.**
INITIALS

_____ **I do not want antibiotics.**
INITIALS

Witness Signature _____ Date: _____

Witness Signature _____ Date: _____

Signed: _____ Date: _____

Address: _____

I have a DNR/Proxy/Living Will On file with

Name: _____ Phone: _____

Check with an Attorney for Living Will or Health Care Proxy needs. This form is not meant to replace a legal document.

Go Bag
In Case of Evacuation

- Copies of important documents, in a waterproof container. Ie., Insurance cards, photo Ids, proof of address, utility bill.
- Extra set of car keys and house keys
- Credit and ATM cards, cash in small bills
- Bottled water and non perishable foods, such as energy or granola bars
- Flashlight, Radio, Batteries
- Your list of medications, and a supply for a few day. Make sure to rotate periodically so the product does not expire.
- First Aid Kit
- Contact and meeting place for your household, and a small map of the area.

IN CASE OF EMERGENCY WALLETICE™ CAN SAVE YOUR LIFE

Statistically 1 out of 5 Americans visit hospital emergency rooms at least once per year! Whether you are 5 years old or 90, if a medical emergency occurs there is a way to help yourself – even if you're unconscious.

Carry WalletICE™. It's a paper that folds up to business card size, and fits easily into your wallet. WalletICE™ contains your vital medical information, and doctors and hospitals find it invaluable in helping them rapidly diagnose you in emergency situations. The information the doctors obtain from WalletICE™ might even save your life!

WalletICE™ gives medical caregivers a snapshot of your medical history so they can make immediate decisions about how to treat you. And it also gives these doctors and hospitals the names of all the people who are able to provide in-depth medical information about you.

Clearly organized and concise, WalletICE™ has multiple lines for you to list all the medications you are taking, and dosages. (And don't forget those over-the-counter medications such as aspirins and supplements you take on a regular basis.) You can also list anything

123

you're allergic to, whom to contact in case of emergency, your doctors and pharmacies and the dates of your hospitalizations.

Also WalletICE™ has designated space to include information that can assist doctors in ascertaining your living wishes if you can't speak for yourself. And there is a place for you to indicate where your Do Not Resuscitate/Health Care Proxy/Living Will are on file.

This helps you avoid heartbreaking situations such as the Terry Shiavo case, in which Ms. Shiavo was brought into an emergency room unconscious, then kept on life supports for years because she had never clearly articulated her end-of-life wishes.

WalletICE™ is also invaluable in helping you monitor your health on a regular basis. It's a perfect place to keep track of your sugar levels if you're a diabetic and your cholesterol levels (HDL–your good cholesterol and LDL–the bad). A doctor may tell you that your blood test is fine. However, if you check your WalletICE™ and see slight changes occurring, you can take the initiative with your doctor or dietitian and discuss changes in your diet or your level of activity.

WalletICE™ has all your medical information organized and within reach. And that means when you go to an emergency room, this neatly folded up piece of paper can talk to your doctors for you, even when you can't speak for yourselves. We carry around a grocery list or a "to do" list to remember all the important things we need. Certainly our health is important enough for us to carry around a "health list," especially since it can save your life.

WalletICE™ is distributed to the public for free, and is supported by local businesses. To find out where WalletICE™ is being distributed in your area, please contact us at annette@walletice.com or give us a call at 347-291-7479

Annette Fisher, President and Executive Director Golden Maturity, Inc., 4210 Surf Avenue, Brooklyn NY 11224 – 347-291-7479

BIOGRAPHIES

Annette Fisher, CSA, SRES®

Annette Fisher has been dedicating her life to helping seniors for over a decade. In addition, she attends continuing education courses on senior issues. She is also a graduate of the IFSA, Institute For Senior Action, a program run by the JASA organization where she completed the program as the class valedictorian. Annette loves giving back to her community and in 2007 she was presented with a Community Service Award, In Recognition of Her Hard Work and Dedication to Finance Education – Region Six High Schools. Most recently, Annette was selected to receive the 2014 Brooklyn Women of Distinction Award given by CNG, Courier News Group Publications and in 2015, she was given an award as Top Women in Business, by the Brooklyn Home Reporter. As if that wasn't enough Annette just received the 2016 Pioneer Award for her Civic Services, from the Merchants of Third Avenue in Bay Ridge Brooklyn.

She is multi licensed as a loan originator – NY & NJ and a real estate salesperson in NY.

At Fort Funding Corp, NMLS 39463, she specializes in reverse mortgages and renovation loans. Annette Fisher, Mortgage Loan Originator, NMLS 67606, is a highly integral part of the processing of reverse mortgages, as well as the liaison between seniors and families, interested in reverse mortgages, title companies, attorneys, financial planners, processors, underwriters, and anyone that needs to be in the communication loop so things run smoothly, most of all for the seniors involved.

Annette is also a Real Estate Salesperson, with a passion focused on helping seniors overcome the stress that might otherwise overwhelm them, when making a transition to a new living space. She works side by side with her clients from start to finish. And, for Annette the finish line has only been reached when her clients eventually move on to their final destiny. Her goal is to help her clients have those remaining years be as sweet as can be. She is the Past President of the Women's Council of Realtors Brooklyn.

Annette is the founder of Golden Maturity, Inc., whose mission is to educate and provide information resources to seniors and their families. The company's first product is WalletICE™. It is a compactly designed and well organized form with space for seniors to list their vital medical information, such as who to contact in case of emergency, their list of medications and any conditions they suffer from. In a medical emergency, even when a senior can't speak for himself or herself, it's hoped

WalletICE™ will save their life! Golden Maturity, Inc. distributes WalletICE™, free to the public.

Annette is also the founder of PESID, (People Empowering Seniors Independence & Dignity). She gets great joy from helping seniors: "I don't have children, but I feel the legacy I leave behind will be my work with seniors. I like being appreciated, and most seniors appreciate you if you really care and can help them. Their world has changed so much: rarely does anyone answer a phone anymore, most so called customer service lines are automated, folks don't seem to have time for conversation. So many seniors have led interesting lives, and they just want someone to understand where they've been and what they know. Also they like working with people who they trust won't just take from them and disappear. That's why being a part of my community has always been so important to me."

If you would like WalletICE™, information on Reverse Mortgages, A Service of Fort Funding Corp. NMLS 39463, Real Estate Home Value Comparisons, A Service of BRESRE Realty Inc, Senior Needs, or if you want to attend a PESID meeting, you can reach Annette Fisher directly at Cell: 347-291-7479.

Robert Howe

Robert Howe is celebrating his law firm's 36th anniversary in Brooklyn. His work focuses on wills, trusts, estates and real estate. He has many senior clients who come to him concerned with having an orderly legal plan to take care of their financial and health care concerns. Robert has assisted hundreds of seniors in drafting wills, health care proxies, powers of attorney and living wills, all essential documents for any senior.

Robert graduated Hamilton College in Utica, New York with a B.A. in government. He graduated Brooklyn Law School in 1981 and is a member in good standing of the New York State Bar.

Robert believes in giving back to his community. He has been president of the Merchants of Third Avenue since 1994. In this capacity, he has worked hard at keeping the avenue cohesive and a vital part of the life of Bay Ridge. He has been involved politically, socially and educationally in many additional aspects of his community.

Debra S. Gross, MS, RD, CDE, CDN, CPT

Debra S. Gross has been a dietitian for over twenty years. She has a Master of Science in clinical nutrition from the City University of New York, Hunter College and a B.S. from Hunter, where she majored in nutrition and food science. She also did an internship at Harlem Hospital as a dietitian.

Debra is a registered dietitian, a certified dietitian nutritionist, a certified diabetes educator and a certified insulin pump trainer. She specializes in diabetes.

Debra opened her private practice focusing on diabetes management in 1996. She has helped thousands of patients understand their diabetes, empowering them to control their blood sugar and avoid or delay complications associated with poor diabetes control. She works alongside endocrinologists and other doctors in New York City and the surrounding areas. Debra provides lectures to professionals, including physicians and nurses (for CME credits). She is also consulted on all nutrition related diseases, as well as alternative nutritional therapies.

Debra has taught as an adjunct professor at City University of New York- Hunter College.

Of great concern to Debra is the misinformation about nutrition that abounds in our society, partially because the word nutritionist and dietitian have come to be used interchangeably:

"Anyone can call themselves a *nutritionist*. Unfortunately, there is absolutely no regulation over using the term. Many nutritionists have no formal education or have taken just a course or two or simply worked in a health food store!

"I decided to become an expert in nutrition once I understood the impact food has on our health. And I undergo yearly continuing education courses to maintain my certifications. Everyone needs to eat, and it is important to have expert information on how we utilize nutrients and how what we eat affects us."

MS Masters of Science, RD Registered Dietitian, CDE certified diabetes educator, CDN certified dietitian nutritionist, CPT certified pump trainer

Debra can be reached at (917) 670-1203
or debraSgross@gmail.com

Marla Loughran, D.C.

Dr. Marla Loughran is a second-generation chiropractor, carrying on the tradition of her mother, Dr. Mary Dadas, who instilled in her children the principles of health and in particular that healing comes from within your body, which is designed to be healthy. Dr. Loughran graduated from New York University in 2001 and the University of Bridgeport, College of Chiropractic in 2008. She then joined her mother's practice in Bay Ridge Brooklyn alongside her brother, Dr. Evan Dadas. When her mother retired, she had been serving the Bay Ridge community almost thirty years. Today Dr. Dadas and Dr. Loughran seek to help their patients heal naturally, safely and effectively from spinal pain. They also lecture frequently on chiropractic topics and ways to have a healthy lifestyle. Dr. Loughran resides in Staten Island, with her husband and children.

Mary Maroney, RN, MSN

Mary Maroney was born in Bay Ridge, Brooklyn into a medical family—her father was a physician at a time

when doctors received $5 for a house call. Nursing and patient care have always been a passion of Mary's.

In 1975, Mary graduated from Wagner College as an RN. She worked for Maimonides Medical Center until 1983, during which time she received her MSN from Adelphi Academy. In 1989, she co-founded *Maxireturn.* The company started as a medical billing company and has expanded to include practice management.

Today *Maxireturn* is in the forefront of assisting hospitals and doctors' offices as well as chiropractic and physical therapy practices with the implementation of Electronic Medical Records. *Maxireturn* helps with all phases of utilizing EMR, from installation and system-wide application through hands-on training of staff. *Maxireturn* also assists with setting up medical billing and scheduling systems.

For consultation on all aspects of implementing EMR or other medical record keeping systems, please contact us at: maxireturn@gmail.com 718-720-7244

Marie Sayour

Marie Sayour has been a caring part of her Bay Ridge Brooklyn community her entire life, growing up there, and returning after studying at the College of Notre Dame to raise her family. Marie was a stay-at-home mom for many years, caring for her three children, including her youngest, Renee, who was born with special needs—and who, Marie is proud to say–is now living with a sense of independence in a group home.

After helping a friend's grandmother with her home care needs, Marie was encouraged to offer this same service to others in the community. Seizing the opportunity to make a difference, RN Staffing Solutions, LLC was born! Initially, four partners planned on offering registered nurses to supplement staff at hospitals as well as to place nurses in homes.

But they recognized a greater need. Seniors and their families really wanted non-medical companions to be placed in seniors' homes to help them with their daily living. Today, RN Staffing Solutions provides services in home, hospital, and nursing home settings with the primary focus on offering non-medical companions to seniors to keep them safe, make sure they have proper nutrition and give them a sense of social connection.

Adult children seek out RN Staffing Solutions because they recognize that their parents or other elderly relatives need a companion to help them. Services are varied and include meal preparation, laundry, light housekeeping, food shopping, help with grooming, and very importantly, pure companionship.

Marie enjoys her time meeting seniors and helping make their lives easier. It is very rewarding work!

For more information, call (718) 720-7242 or email rnstaffingsolutions@gmail.com.

Feel free to reach out to the authors

of

Seniors Get Your Ducks In A Row.

We look forward to speaking with the community.

Publisher: Golden Maturity Inc. 347-291-7479

SeniorsGetYourDucksInARow.com

Made in the USA
Middletown, DE
07 March 2017